Games & Activities
for the Cooperative Classroom

Written by Lynn Molyneux
Illustrated by Tom Heffernan and Pam Marasco
Cover art by Pam Marasco
Typesetting by Nicol Walters

CONTENTS

Games & Activities
For The
Cooperative Classroom
A How-To for Integrating Cooperative Learning, Games & The Content Areas

Games & Activities For The Cooperative Classroom differs in one sure way from all other cooperative learning books : This book contains the stuff that you and your students actually WANT to do.

In **Games & Activities For The Cooperative Classroom** you will not find plans for *Simon Says* or pages to copy, cut and color. You will find progressive ideas, information and plans for *Chain Reaction,* for *Magic Number* and for *We The People.* This book TELLS ALL. It's the low-down on getting acquainted. It's the mystery of thinking finally exposed. It's communication, problem solving and curriculum integration all tied up together.

All of our books place emphasis on active learning- learning by exploring, analyzing, applying, questioning, discussing, and evaluating in a real-world context. Anyone alert to current research in education will not be surprised by such language. They illustrate the notion of teaching for understanding. We think **Games & Activities For The Cooperative Classroom** covers this ground in an especially satisfying way.

The activities are organized around the areas of language arts, mathematics, social studies and science. They bridge skills and content in meaningful, fun strategies. As you may have suspected, they call on kids to engage in thought-demanding productions together.

Help bring out your students' best and create a collaborative classroom where everyone learns. These 144 pages of all-star kid and teacher approved activities and games will astound and deliver.

Serious Fun!!
Thought provoking
insightful ways to
Reach kids!!
Active Learning!!
Current!!

Chapter One
A Perfunctory Look at the Merits of Cooperative Learning

Cooperative learning is an area where Murphy's Law often rules- and the worst case scenarios read like tragicomedies. Students are passive when they need to interact actively- with each other, the teacher and the resources. High-level thinking, problem solving, self- explanation, discussion, peer-teaching, project-based learning and the use of authentic problems with real-world significance are the exception. Multiple perspectives are nowhere to be seen. Hurricanes and thunder storms make surprise appearances, as does the "*boredom bug.*" And yet, experimentation is everywhere and the recurrent theme in the research on cooperative learning is overwhelming; it WORKS. Cooperative learning in all its ebullient variety...

* leads to higher academic achievement and greater productivity. The more students collaborate, the more they will learn and remember.
* is more real world. Collaborative experiences in an environment that reinforce the notions of *"We're all in this together!"* or *"Two heads are better than one!"* help students learn to share responsibility for learning, help students learn to organize themselves and help them learn to demonstrate their understandings.
* encourages all students to rise to the challenge of higher expectations. Students appreciate each other's talents and intellectual pecking orders are discouraged. *"All students can learn."*

So, it seems only appropriate that we devote an entire book to an incredibly multifaceted, most exhilarating and sometimes confusing and maddening approach- c o o p e r a t i v e   l e a r n i n g .

What Makes Cooperative Learning Click

The sights, sounds, smells, thoughts and feelings sallying forth from your classroom are about to be transformed. Let us explain. From the first day of school and everyday thereafter, you and your students form and build a community- a wonderfully positive context for learning. You move deliberately into the cooperative process by preparing students to work together. It happens in a number of ways:

1) Implementing the Getting Acquainted Activities
These ideas link language arts, science and math. They are presented throughout the chapters that follow and help set the tone for smooth sailing throughout the year. Collaborative vs. adversarial relationships are developed as students feel comfortable to share ideas, to take risks, to debate and to explore alternate points of view.

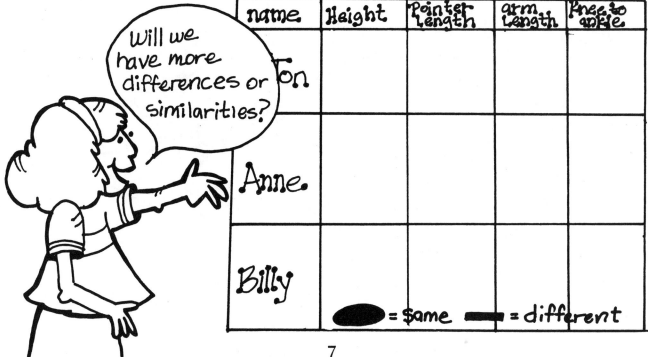

2) Creating Cooperative Standards

When it comes to classroom management, teachers of cooperative classrooms fare better than ever. The skills of leadership, decision making, communication, knowing and valuing others, settling disagreements and expressing support have to be taught so that students know and understand what is expected of them. As these skills start clicking, students will be better equipped to regulate their own behavior and become more responsible for their learning.

⇨ 1. Identify the behavior standard. Connect it to a previous experience

⇨ 2. Help your students see the need for their behavior. How will it benefit them? When should it be used?

⇨ 3. Demonstrate, model, diagram, map, act out, illustrate and define the behavior.

⇨ 4. Practice, monitor and guide the students as they master the behavior.

⇨ 5. Implement debriefing.

⇨ 6. Encourage. Distribute the practice.

3) Recognizing Individual Differences Among Students

Believe that you can deal with the needs of the individual children within a cooperative framework. Bring out your students' best by making positive interdependence work as well for you as it did for the Patriot soldiers during the Revolutionary War. *I am as responsible for my own learning as I am for the members of my team."* Commit to individual accountability, face-to-face interaction and group processing. We're talking motivation, inspiration, plain fun, engagement and just plain results here.

4) Knowing Your Students, Their Personalities and Their Learning Styles

Another requisite for success in building a cooperative classroom is that teachers provide inherently interesting and challenging learning activities that use other alternative approaches so that all students are reached. Thematic, interdisciplinary units, differentiation of the curriculum, learning centers, curriculum compacting, independent projects, and an infusion of critical and creative thinking into subject matter instruction all connect with the goals and principles of cooperative learning. Finally, research has found that teachers of cooperative learning who *do it right* balance cooperative activities with individualized and competitive strategies.

• Linguistic • Mathematical • Visual-Spatial • Body Kinesthetic • Musical •

5) Staging, Designing and Establishing The Most Cooperative Classroom That Kids Will Ever See and Be Part Of

On the theory that what this world really needs is a whole lot more compassion, communication, appreciation for diversity, emotional expression and cooperation, we're all for kids creating bulletin boards, mobiles, learning centers, posters, taped messages, tie-dyed T-shirts, T-charts, dioramas, displays...we could go on, but you get the idea. Hold community meetings, establish goals for the week, the month and the year and involve parents and other community resources.

And, in response to the harsh realities of teacher-overload, we are providing here a crucial list of elements that are research validated, teacher-friendly and integral to a cooperative approach.

a. *focus on generative topics*
b. *develop content goals for topics around key understandings and principles*
c. *emphasize self-explanation*
d. *connect critical & creative thinking skills to subject matter instruction*

e. *help students construct meaning through problem and project-based learning*

f. *use (and love) performance assessments that give you, your students, parents and everyone a truer picture of what students know and can do*

g. *bowl everyone over with authentic problems*

h. *play favorites with the big T, standing for technically thoughtful and meaning that **thinking** is the foundation which supports instructional decisions and engages students and you in **active construction**- developing knowledge by linking and integrating students' pre-existing knowledge to new information*

Engage the young, old and the restless in creating a cooperative classroom where kids learn to respect each others' differences, to see beyond stereotyped labels and learn to live in a multicultural society.

The Art and Craft of Cooperative Groups

We'll start with stark realism.

*Cooperative groups are determined by the nature of the task.

*To be just, you need to consider how skilled your students are in interpersonal and small group skills so that they can coordinate their efforts in larger, cooperative groups.

*Students of widely divergent skills and talents and of different gender, race, religious, socioeconomic or economic backgrounds need to interact with each other.

*Self-segregation should happen (at least once in a while).

*Groups that stay together long enough to bond become successful, powerful and totally responsible.

*Feel confident about altering the sizes of groups so that students work in pairs, in groups of three, in groups of four and even in groups of five or six.

*Stress the philosophy and theories behind cooperative learning as it's being practiced.

*Groups and group members need to have, from the very beginning, a clear understanding of what is to be learned and how that learning will be assessed.

In our continuing effort to maintain a paper chase, we also deem that rewarding completion of tasks is important and that assigning specific roles for students to perform can also facilitate learning. Assigning complementary roles to each group member, if appropriate to the task, also increases the odds for positive interdependence. Here, straight from the Trellis archives, are a few of the roles that specify the responsibilities a group might need in order to achieve: speaker, scribe, controller, manager, broadcaster, elaborator, summarizer, timekeeper and encourager. For obvious reasons, group names (superheroes, beasties, card sharks, decoders, boondogglers, jesters, top hats, ladybugs and the wizards) can also develop camaraderie.

There are many effective strategies that emphasize group cooperation and social skill development. Models such as Think, Pair & Share (Lyman and McTighe 1988), Numbered Heads Together (Kagan 1990), Roundtable, Jigsaw (Aronson 1978), Teammates Consult (Kagan 1990) and Team-Up (Kagan 1990) all speak to the differentiation of tasks and processes. For anyone who wants some crystal-clear help with these blueprints for cooperative learning, the other Trellis books in the series should definitely do the trick.

If you revel in adventure, you've got the spirit. If you yearn for a world where individual differences are respected and appreciated and where everyone collaborates, you've got the interest. And, most importantly, if you've ever found yourself harmonizing along on *We All Sing With The Same Voice*, you've got the idea.

"Whatever you can do, or dream you can, begin it. Boldness has genius, and magic in it." -Goethe

About The Games & Activities

Playing: *You Can't Do Too Much Of It*

It isn't whether you win or lose but how you act, react, feel, think and create. The distinctive feature of **Games & Activities For The Cooperative Classroom** is the emphasis on social skills. Every idea encourages helpful and fun-filled interaction as students investigate, inquire, solve problems, make decisions, apply knowledge, make meaning, connect with the real world and talk happily. The *events* are centered around the content areas of math, social studies, language arts and science so that students ...

1. Have the opportunity to explain what they know and what they are learning. When students share their generalizations, applications, what-ifs, questions and understandings, it's an "understanding performance."

2. Can seek out information using a variety of resources including literature and the computer.

3. Tackle meaningful problems that are rich in contextual detail and that lend themselves to authentic assessment.

4. Engage in higher-level thinking by analyzing, applying, critiquing, defending, asking, debating, synthesizing and evaluating.

5. Take risks, give-it-a-go, make messes, pace themselves, think in other ways and learn.

6. PLAY. It can't be the eyes on the prize that make children love games and activities. Is it incurable optimism, a compulsive gambling streak or just the thrill of the sport? Maybe the need to play comes from the doodling brain cells in the human brain right next to the rolling dice section of the cerebellum. *"What's with this game obsession?"* we asked our favorite class of grade-schoolers and a select group of not-so-forthcoming adults. Their answers were simple: *"The dare of it all...It's learning and fun all rolled up together...They're what we WANT to do...You do stuff, not stare or listen."* So there! These games and activities are meant to be done.

Turn to your partner and...
- decide together what you liked best about this activity.
- Think of an idea that would make it more fun.
- explain how you were able to help eachother.
- explain how this activity helped you better understand predators and prey.

These games and activities are destined to help your students "connect things up." Cooperative learning, in a game context, can be a powerful delivery system for teaching and learning science, social studies, language arts or math. It can bring out everyone's best as they Spell That Word, play Prime Time or About Face. We want you and your students to become committed players.

Chapter Two
Language Arts & Cooperative Games & Activities

You know that language arts integrates the processes of listening, speaking, writing and reading as one total operation rather than as isolated subjects to be taught and learned. What you might not know is how much of a cooperative enterprise language arts actually is. It's about opportunities for oral language (discussions, debates, drama,); for writing experiences (listing, charting, learning logs); for listening experiences (read aloud) and for reading experiences (shared reading). Working collaboratively affords children occasions to use language as a tool to solve problems, apply knowledge, think through topics carefully, share the responsibility for learning something, build understandings, explore alternative points of view and rethink their ideas.

We feel confident that you'll like the learning, the teaching and the fun that goes on when you use the games and activities in this chapter. And, we know that you'll appreciate the interdisciplinary connections. Adapt, extend or redesign them. Life won't be the same.

Memory Serves

This game for groups of four, five or six gives students an opportunity to become acquainted and to practice communication skills. To do the activity, students must practice active listening. This will be the highlight of your day. Take your class outdoors...substitute water balloons for balls...Play it for a week and explore a different topic each day. Vary the teams.

Materials
Koosh balls, bean bags, foam balls,etc.
stop watch or timer

Directions
1. Form groups.
2. Introduce the game. *"Today, you're going to discover the many ways that you are the same. First, form a circle. Pass the ball back and forth to your group members. Each time you pass the ball, call out (where you vacationed this summer, the title of your favorite book, ways you have fun, jobs you have to do at home, etc.). You will pass the ball for two minutes. Exactly. When the timer sounds, the fun begins. Now each time you pass the ball you must remember and name what the person to whom you are passing the ball said. If you forget, just ask, "What do you ...like on your pizza?"*
3. Bring everyone together. *"What made it easy for you to remember what your teammates said? What did you enjoy about the Memory Serves? What surprises did you discover? What common ground do you and your classmates share?"*
4. Vary this activity by adding more balls. Make Venn diagrams or have students write about this activity in their learning logs: Name three ways you and your classmates are the same. Name three ways you and your classmates are different. Sketch and color a picture illustrating Memory Serves.

Page-Turning Fun

In this collaborative activity, students share the responsibility for writing a chant, finger play, song, short story or a poem and must organize themselves and the topic to do it well. Roundtable gives a group project new life!

Materials

paper
pencils, pens, colored pencils

Directions

1. Determine a topic on which students are to write. Compose a title or an opener. It can be written on the chalkboard or on individual sheets of paper. You need as many sheets of paper as you have groups.
2. Form groups of four, five or six.
3. Distribute one sheet of paper and one pencil to each group.
4. Introduce the activity. *"We have learned a mega- amount of information about butterflies. Today, your task is to share what you know about butterflies. Let's think of all the ways we might share our information. What forms can writing take?"* List students' ideas on the board. Discuss the pieces of writing with which students are most familiar. *"In your groups, decide what form your writing will take. The first writer creates a topic (sentence). Then, each team member contributes a line and then passes it to the next person in your group. The paper goes around and around until each person has written at least one line about butterflies."*
5. Monitor each group's progress. Encourage complimentary talk. *"Doesn't it make you feel good to hear Cecile tell you she liked your idea, Jane?"*
6. Ask teams to share their pieces.
7. Implement group processing. *"How did you decide what to write? What make it easy for your group to create a chant, Nancy? In what ways was it easy for you to finish the poem, Conor?"*
8. Extend this activity. Ask the second writer to read the first sentence and write his/her sentence below it. Then, he folds the paper so that the first sentence is hidden and only his sentence can be read. The paper is passed to the third (fourth, fifth, etc.) writer who follows the same procedure. When everyone has contributed, the paper is unfolded and the story is read aloud to the group and then to the class. Surprise, surprise!

Razzmatazz

...and all that jazz. This cooperative activity will add some madcap fun and bang-up action to your day when students reconstruct the BIG ideas of a story, a topic or a zany experience.

Materials
large strips of paper
felt-tipped markers, crayons, colored pencils
tape

Directions
1. Determine an important concept that you want students to review, relearn or understand. Discuss the topic. *"Yesterday we investigated liquids. Who remembers what happened when we added a drop of red food coloring to the jar containing water and corn oil?"* Discuss. *"What else did you learn that you didn't know?"* Etc. *"Today, in groups of four, we're going to write to help us rethink our ideas and to cement our learning."*
2. Divide your class into groups of four.
3. Assign the roles of facilitator, recorder, reader and reporter. Distribute a paper strip and marker to each group.
4. Write a topic sentence on the chalkboard. Talk your way through it. *"Discuss your ideas about the thickness and density of liquids. Sort them out. Write one sentence that is about the BIG idea and that is in your own words."*
5. Monitor each group's progress. *"How did your group decide to prove the sentence on the board, C.J.?" "Everyone in your group established eye contact as you read, Jim."*
6. Have each reporter attach and read his/her group's sentence below the first sentence.
7. Read the finished product orally. Rearrange the sentences if appropriate. Herald the creative group process!
8. Implement group processing. *"How did your group decide what was important to remember? What made it easy for your group to expand the topic sentence? How were you able to share ideas and information?"* Compare the results. *"In what ways are these ideas alike?"* Etc.
9. According to the research, the writing portion of this activity should take no more than ten minutes if you want more meaningful, detailed summaries.
10. Extend this activity by designing this activity for each group. Or, have groups write questions rather than statements.

Writing Workout

Writing Workout uses the strategy of Roundtable and can be played by groups of three, four or five. It gives students an opportunity to generate many possible answers and to think about what they know. It can be used with any subject area. Here, the activity is geared to help students create a sense of community and understand the ties that bind.

Materials

a timer or a stopwatch
paper
pencils, felt-tipped markers, colored pencils

Directions

1. Form groups.
2. Distribute one pencil and one paper to each group.
3. Introduce the activity. *"Today, your group's task is to list the many, varied people, places and professions that make up a community. Each member of your group will write one idea on the paper and then pass it to the person sitting next to him. The paper goes around the group for three minutes. Exactly."*
4. *"How many answers do you think your group can come up with? Talk about it and write your best guess at the top of the paper before you start."*
5. Have each group report their results. Record groups' answers on a large chart. (Use a different colored marker for each group.) Discuss the findings. *"In what ways are your lists the same? In what ways are they different?"*
6. Summarize the experience. *"How were you able to write so many answers? How close was your estimate to the actual number of answers you came up with? Why do you think so? Did you feel you had enough time? Did timing this activity help? In what ways? Etc."*
7. Extend this activity by sorting the lists according to the places, professions and people that also found in your school or classroom.
8. You can also have students list ways a community meets people's needs, resources of communities, places in a community for kids, animals, fun and so on.

We, The People

We, The People gets kids thinking about those specific behaviors that you and your students outlined at the beginning of the year as the five guiding rules or principles for your classroom. It assumes that children have had a voice in establishing these standards. To do this Corner (Kagan 1990) activity, students have to think critically, defend their choice(s), explore alternative points of view, listen and speak.

Materials

construction paper or tagboard for signs
felt-tipped markers
string for hanging (or easels)
chart paper

Directions

1. Create signs upon which each rule is written and qualify it in some way so as to invite critical thinking. Post one at each corner (or a different area) of your classroom.
2. Present the activity by drawing attention to and reading each sign. Give students time to consider each one. *"We're going to use Corners to find out how we feel about our class rules. With which statement do you most agree? Think about it for a minute and then go to the corner for the answer that you think is best."*
3. Within the corners, have students pair up to explain their reasoning and ideas. *"Find a partner in your group and discuss why you chose the statement you did. Use voices that won't disturb others. Listen to your partner's reasons for his opinion(s). What reasons can you offer? Share your ideas."*
4. Circulate. If a corner group is too large, form groups of four within the big group.
5. Ask individual students from each corner to explain their opinions to the class. *"Defend your choice."*
6. Implement group processing. *" What was easy about sharing your opinions? Did anyone change groups?"*
7. Extend this activity by reading <u>Sam Johnson and the Blue Ribbon Quilt</u> by Lisa Campbell (Lothrop, 1983).

Box-It

Challenge your students to be fluent, to think with what they know in order to demonstrate and build their understandings and their vocabulary. According to Carroll (1964), *"The teaching of words, and the meaning and concepts they designate or convey, is one of the principal tasks of teachers at all levels of education."* This activity is for any place, any time zone and any kid.

Materials

paper- go big, go really BIG
colored pencils, felt-tipped markers, crayons

Directions

1. Determine a subject area with which you want this activity to connect. What vocabulary do you want to reinforce and have your students truly learn?
2. Divide your class into groups of two or three.
3. Each pair receives one sheet of chart paper and two different colored markers.
4. Assign the roles of readers and recorders (and elaborators).
5. Ask the recorders to write the title (subject area, topic, etc.) at the top of their charts. *"Draw a five square by five square grid on the chart paper."* Demonstrate.
6. Introduce the activity. *"During this week's reading of Danny the Champion of the World by Roald Dahl, we noted many descriptive words and phrases. Yesterday, you wrote a short list of the ones you liked in your learning logs. Today, we're going to use these words and others to play Box-It. Here's how. First, choose a marker to use throughout the game. The object of Box-It is to fill the paper with many words. To do this, take turns writing words from ... in the boxes. Each time you write a word you must use it in a sentence. Your partner has to agree that you are using it correctly. Then it's your partner's turn. Help each other. Give each other encouragement. Use the Powerful Positive Words posted on our class chart. When all pairs are finished, we'll share the finished products."*

Rajah	three	wise	ideas	
ruler	truth	wanderer	ideal	
right	trunk	wary	India	
	tusk	warning	imagine	
	talk			

Royal

7. Circulate as pairs work to complete their grids. *"How did you decide that Nancy's sentence demonstrates meaning, Pat? I like the way you helped Meghan with her sentence, Karen. I just heard Allan say, "That's a great idea." How many of you are using positive statements for encouragement?"*

8. Implement group processing. *"What did you do in your groups of two to encourage and help each other? How did it feel when you helped?"*

9. Talk about the wild palette of completed grids. *"What makes all these grids alike? In what ways are they connected?"*

10. Extend this activity. Have students write a pertinent word down the side of the boxes. All the words in that row have to begin with the side letter. Make it even more complicated by writing categories at the top of the columns.

Chain Reaction

Chain Reaction is a variation of Box-It. They're both like eating popcorn-students can sit there and munch, no play, away.

Materials

big sheets or strips of paper, adding machine tape
felt-tipped markers, colored pencils, crayons

Directions

1. Divide your class into groups of three or four. Distribute a paper and markers to each group.
2. Discuss the topic, theme, etc. that you want this activity to reinforce.
3. *"The object of this game is to create a long, long chain of words that explains or describes_____. The first player writes a word. On his turn, he uses it in a sentence. The second player thinks of a word relating to the topic that begins with the last letter of the first player's word and records it. Everytime a word is written, the player uses it in a sentence. Your group members have to agree that you've used it correctly. You are to help each other if you get stuck."* Demonstrate.
4. *"How many words do you think your group can come up with? Make a guess. Talk about it and then start creating your chain. The game is over when you can't write anymore because you've run out of words! Make interesting chains. Weave them all over your paper. Think about intersections and expressways!"* Encourage students to use capital letters, bold, dark, light, rhythmic, angular, curved, thick and thin letters, underlining and color to make their chains unique.
5. Monitor each pair's progress. Encourage the use of positive statements. Revel in students' personal learnings as they develop, cement and extend their understandings about the topic.
6. Discuss the results. Talk about students' ideas. *"Let's learn from each other's thinking. What positive statements did you use to help each other? What did you like about this game? How accurate were your guesses? What was hard about figuring out what words to write?"*
7. *"You know a lot about....! Let's display these learning creations."*

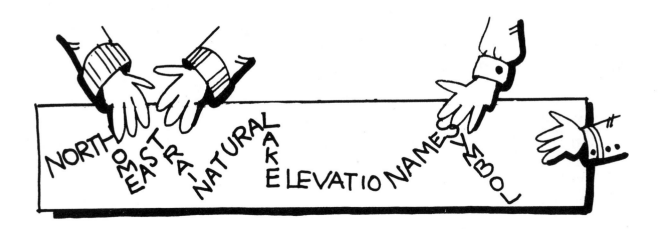

Using Literature

There are some things in life that are simply too important to scrimp on. Like enjoying and exploring literature while building rich, vital understandings of concepts. The evidence tells us that experiences in language arts are most likely to determine the fate of our students. Finger plays, chants, poems, big books, trade books and songs are serious pieces of life-saving equipment. Which is why we give literature the best that Trellis has to give on the following pages. The activities are generic. They're supercharged. They'll lift everyone's spirits. Go with them.

Poetry Power

_____ voices are better than one. Get ready to shake up the poetry scene in your classroom. Poetry Power revives the spoken word with true kid power and originality. It will also help students join forces to know effective communication as well as practice active listening.

Activity 1- Reading Poetry

Materials
a myriad of poetry (for read aloud, independent reading, shared reading and choral reading)
recordings of the spoken word
chart paper
crayons, felt-tipped markers, colored pencils
tape recorders, video equipment

Directions
1. Gather some excellent poetry for read aloud that speaks to the theme your class is studying. Write the poem(s) on chart paper or on transparencies.
2. Divide your class into groups. The number of students in each group depends on the particular poem.

3. *"In your groups of (three), take turns sharing what you think poetry is about. What makes some poems speak to you? What do you remember the most about the collections of poetry that we've read about mammals?"* Etc.

4. Ask groups to share their thoughts with the class. Discuss.

5. Introduce the task. *"Today we are going to experiment with different ways of reading several poems."*

6. Display the poem. Read it aloud. Enjoy the sounds and the rhythms of the language.

7. *"This poem can be divided into _____parts. Look at how the words are stacked. Let's find the repeated phrases and lines together."* Encourage students to help you. Elicit ideas about syncopated rhythms, explosions of sound, etc. *"Where does it make sense to break this up?"*

8. Assign or have groups choose sections for oral reading or chanting.

9. *"Practice reading your parts. Add gestures for dramatic emphasis. Share your ideas. Go for originality."*

10. Observe groups working. Ask questions such as, *"How is your group taking turns offering ideas?"*

11. Hold a poetry reading. *"Let's make this poem come alive. Let's hear it."*

12. Zero in on what worked. *"Each group varied the tempo. It made absolute sense."* Etc.

13. Implement group processing. *"What made it easy for you to chant your part of this poem? How were you able to synchronize your voices? How did your group decide to add clapping?"*

14. Facilitate other experiences. Have groups vary the pitches and/or volumes of their voices. Add musical instruments. Make the parts staccato. Have groups illustrate their parts, create variations or add new verses.

15. Have students summarize this activity in their learning logs. Provoke student thinking with prompts that get them operating on several levels.

  a. What is your favorite version of _____? What did you like about it?

  b. What patterns did you find in these choral readings?

  c. In what ways did our readings sound like music? Name at least two ways.

  d. Think about the sounds of our reading. Name at least one piece of music that it was like.

  e. In what ways does choral reading make poetry come alive? Name at least two ways.

16. These books might help you get started.

  Earth Verses and Water Rhymes by J. Patrick Lewis (Atheneum, 1991)

  Sing a Song of Popcorn by Beatrice Schenk de Regniers, et al. (Scholastic, 1988)

  Whiskers & Rhymes by Arnold Lobel (Greenwillow, 1986)

  Happy Birthday by Lee Bennett Hopkins (Simon & Schuster, 1991)

  Eric Carle's Animals Animals selected by Eric Carle (Scholastic, 1989)

  The Random House Book of Poetry for Children selected by Jack Jack Prelutsky (Random House, 1983)

Activity 2- Writing Poetry

A love of poetry, in all its forms, is partially dictated by the climate of your classroom. Share and enjoy it with your class. Expose your class to poetry from other cultures. Survey your students to discover their preferences and their favorite poets. Create cross-curricular activities that extend favorite poems & themes. Here we suggest a collaborative way to link students' experiences and knowledge with their poetic language.

Directions

1. Form partners. *"What is a map (a web, cluster, etc.)? Share your ideas with your partners."*
2. Discuss students' ideas. Record their thoughts as a map. Point out the connections. Emphasize the elaborations with different colors.

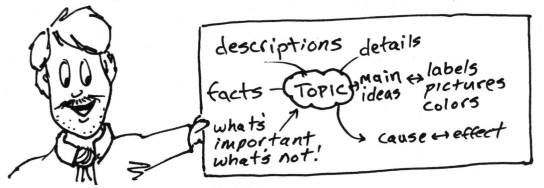

3. Introduce the task. *"Today we are going to play with our ideas, experiences, knowledge, curiosities, and thoughts about _____."*
4. Model the process. Verbalize and web your ideas and knowledge about _____. Uncover words and phrases that connote knowing and caring about the topic. Then play with the results. Emphasize the repetition, the form, the pattern, etc. depending on how your writing develops. Stop occasionally. *"What do you think?"*
5. Invite each pair to follow the same procedure. Assigning roles will help structure the activity.
   Writer- This student records.
   Reader- This student reads and rereads the ideas until the
           piece is finished.
6. *"Which groups would like to read their pieces?"* Have the class offer positive comments. *"What worked? What did you like?"* Etc.
7. Implement group processing. *"In what ways did your roles help you with your writing? What could you do to improve the way you worked together the next time? Did you map first?"*

8. Students may wish to include these pieces in their portfolios.
9. Ask them to write about the experience in their learning logs.
   a. Respond to this statement. *"Poetry is like music."*
   b. Name three attributes that all poetry shares.
   c. Finish this thought. Working with a partner.....
   d. Identify one thing that worked in your poem.

Activity 3- Trade Books

Join in a celebration of the many types of literature. Use this menu of ideas to help extend your students' knowledge and understanding of a topic and to offer literary enjoyment. Include fiction and non-fiction, picture books and magazines in your repertoire.

Directions

1. Divide your students into groups of two or three. Ask team members to share information about their favorite book.
2. Assign roles to help structure the activity, when appropriate.
   Writer- This team player records!
   Reader-This team player reads and rereads the ideas from beginning to end.
   Materials Organizer- This team player is responsible for the necessary materials.
3. Present the task. Choose from the following menu. Adapt them to meet the needs of your students. Think about learning styles.
4. Accommodate group processing at the end of each activity. *"What words of encouragement did your group use? How did you stay in your roles? What did you do to discover the answers to your own questions? What did you to to help your group? Name one way you helped."* Etc.

a. <u>A Puzzle Of a Story</u>- Use the reproducible found page 32 to make Tangram puzzles. Duplicate different puzzles (use wild colors) and place separate Tangrams in envelopes or packets. Each trio should have one puzzle. Have groups cut out the puzzle pieces and then create a puzzle to represent the literature read. Compare the puzzle to a story map. Remind students to think about events, problems, setting, ending, characters, etc. You might also discuss the patterns found in many stories.

b. <u>Rantings and Ravings</u>- *"I am what I am."* Many characters (real & fictional) are remembered for their words. In this activity, groups search and locate important quotations and then share them with the class. Discuss an easily remembered quote such as, *"Not by the hair of my chinny, chin chin!"* Talk about why the quotation is famous or important. Does it imply a conflict? Is it timeless? Is it just plain fun? Then have groups identify various quotes from books they've read and create scripts, puppets, illustrations or re-enactments to share with the class.

c. <u>Technically Speaking</u>- We know that kids need plenty of opportunities to think about the content they're learning. One way it can happen is to engage them in paraphrasing. Have students select a passage (or assign each group a section). Then ask group members to take turns paraphrasing. You can also invite group members to divide the material so that each student is responsible for a portion of the content. Together, the group produces a written or oral version of the entire selection to share with the class.

d. <u>Short Over Long</u>- Short Over Long prompts students to engage in self-explanation and thinking-centered learning. Prepare a list of cues that will facilitate students' interpretations of the literature. Glean the main ideas of the text. Write short statements or information on index cards, paper, etc. Have groups retell everything they remember from their reading. *"Take turns sharing events, ideas, etc. that you remember. Listen to the ideas of your team members. Elaborate on their ideas. When you can't give any more information, the materials managers should come up and get a cue card. Read the cues. They should help you remember other things from your reading."* Discuss the results. *"In what ways did the cue cards help? How did you organize yourselves so that you covered everything in the reading?"*

e. <u>Authentic</u>- Summarizing is the next step after paraphrasing. In this activity, each group member produces a written or recorded summary after the entire group has discussed the salient points of the text. Then the summaries are compared and contrasted. *"In what ways was your summary different from Jane's, Ray? In what ways was it the same?"* The differences in the students' interpretations can be plotted on an H chart. Etc.

f. <u>Putting It All Together</u>- Here is yet another tactic to get students thinking about content carefully. Select material that can be cut into paragraphs. Duplicate and cut out the passage(s). Mix the cut paragraphs up so that the material is out of sequence. Place in an envelope or packet. Give one envelope to each group. Present the task. Readers read the paragraphs. Together, the group members decide how to sequence the paragraphs so that the material makes sense. The Materials Managers place the strips in the correct (or agreed upon) sequence. In this activity, the writer can take on the role of Encourager. Each group then reads their product to the class. Discuss the results. *"How did your groups reach agreement?"* Prepare different material for each group. Rotate the envelopes.

g. <u>Fusion</u>- Have groups create a rap about selected material. It could be tape recorded or videoed for the class.

h. <u>Chart It</u>- Groups of three can identify critical vocabulary words and create large charts to classify them. Words that tell Where, Number Words, Words that Tell About ..., Describing Words, Foreign or Colloquial Language, Words That We Use, Synonyms, Etc.

i. <u>Readers Theater</u>- Material that contains substantial dialogue, several characters and a strong structure lends itself to dramatic reenactments or mini-dramas. Have each group choose a story to act out. Then ask each group to identify the setting, character roles, etc. *"Bring the story to life. Talk about and discover the elements that need to be portrayed."* Require that all group members act in the minidrama. Allow time for practice. Each group could present their script live, video it or record it. Have everyone get in touch with their imagination by using body puppets for storytelling- thumb puppets, knee puppets, toe puppets...

Tangram Puzzle Pieces

What happens when cooperative groups are given Tangram puzzles? They go to pieces. Tangrams capture the twists and turns of cooperative learning. Students have to follow directions, share, come to agreement, listen...and love learning together.

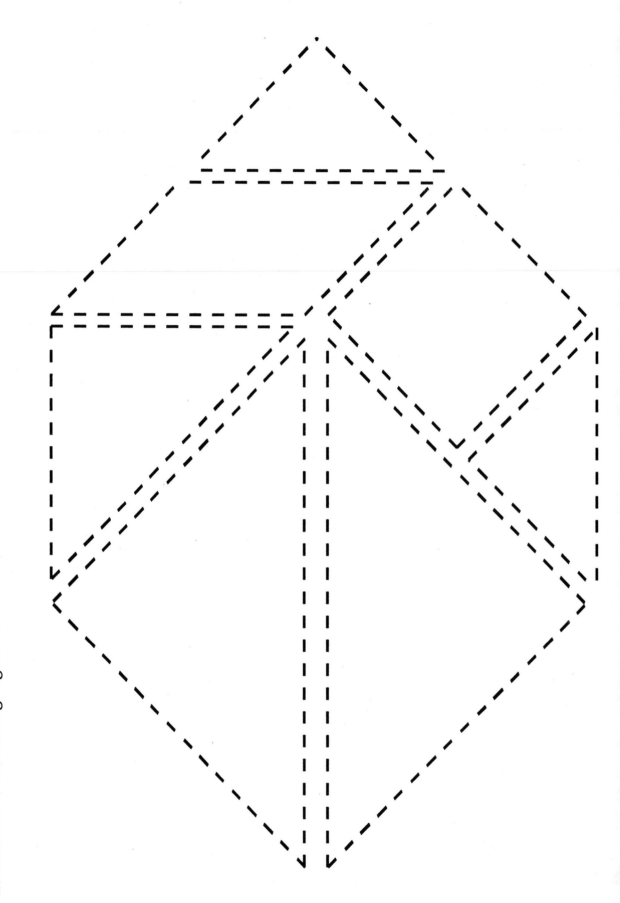

Putting A Spin On Spelling-I

Copying this week's spelling words ten times each can be tormenting. We have a deep sympathy for that kind of torture. We have thought about different ways to approach the problem. We know that if we want our students to grow as writers and readers, spelling if taught as a process, can have an enduring impact. So, here's what we ended up with: three events that will reinforce spelling consciousness. Putting A Spin On Spelling can be played in groups of two. It asks students to listen, to stay on task, to interact and to evaluate.

Materials

pencils
fun stuff: Cuisinaire rods, pattern blocks, dental floss, yarn, ribbons, string, macaroni, trays of sand, beads, etc.
books & magazines
stop watches or timers
copies of the Put A Spin On Spelling reproducible

Directions

1. Form groups.
2. Introduce the activity. *"Today, you are going to practice your spelling words. In your groups, you will take turns writing the words that are really giving you trouble from this week's spelling list. The spin is to write them with... Cuisinaire rods. You and your partner will time each other."*
3. Distribute materials. Each pair receives a recording sheet, a timer, fun stuff with which to write, paper and pencil.
4. *"Let the games begin. First, discuss which words you and your partner need to review (learn). Write them down on the recording sheet. Then, take turns writing each one with (the rods). You will also take turns being timers. Make sure that your buddy can read the words you write."* Etc.
5. Monitor each pair's progress. *"I'm struck by how quiet Tom's group is working."*
6. Have each pair report their results.
7. Implement group processing. *"What effect did timing your practice have? Why do you think your time improved as you went down the list?"*
8. Post the times.

Putting A Spin On Spelling-II
Speed Reading

Materials
literature (including magazines)
pencils
copies of the Putting A Spin On Spelling reproducible
stop watchers or timers

Directions
1. Divide your class into pairs.
2. Introduce the activity. *"Today we're going to practice our spelling words. In your groups, you will take turns searching for and finding the spelling rogues that are giving you trouble from this week's list. You and your partner will time each other."*
3. Distribute the materials. Each pair receives a recording sheet, a timer and a pencil. Literature needs to be available for each group as well.
4. *"Decide which words you want to practice. Write them down on the recording sheet. Make sure you reach agreement. Then, take turns finding the words. Open a book or magazine and see how long it takes your to locate your spelling rogues. Time each other."* Etc. Partners should use different books.
5. Monitor each group's progress. *"How did you decide to use the National Geographic, Caroline?"*
6. Have each pair report their results.
7. Implement group processing. *"How did you reach agreement on your word lists? Did you each contribute interesting words to the list? What was easy about this activity? Did you visual memory help? In what ways?"*

Putting A Spin On Spelling-III
Back Spelling

Materials

pencils
stop watches or timers
copies of the Back Spelling reproducible

Directions

1. Follow the same procedure as for the previous two activities.
2. In Back Spelling, pairs take turns writing the spelling words from their combined lists on each other's back. The partner whose back upon the word is being written has to guess what the word is. *"How long will it take for your partner to figure out what word you wrote? Time how long it takes you to guess the words that are being written on your backs. Try it!"*
3. Distribute the materials. Each pair receives a recording sheet, a timer and a pencil.
4. Circulate. *"I like the way you and Matt are encouraging each other, Nicol."*
5. Have each pair report their progress. *"Did you and your partner's time come close for any of the words you practiced? Was it tempting to peek at the stop watch?"*
6. Implement group processing. *"How did you organize yourselves? How did you decide who would go first? Was it fun?"*
7. Post the times. Discuss how this activity used students' bodies and kinesthetic memories.

Putting A Spin On Spelling-IV
Beat The Clock

Fame should have a master division, like tennis, for teachers who have stuck it out, a la Mrs. Rogers, laughing and believing in active learning for years. Her advice: *"take your class outdoors for this special activity."* Liberate those *"I need to be a little loud sometimes "*vocal chords.

Materials

pencil
balls (Koosh balls, rubber balls, foam balls, etc.)
stop watches or timers
copies of the Beat The Clock recording sheet

Directions

1. Divide your class into groups of three.
2. Present the activity. *"In your groups of three, talk about the spelling words that are giving you the most trouble. Which words are you finding it impossible to learn with either your auditory or visual memory?"*
3. *"Today we're going to learn with our kinesthetic memories"* Discuss how our kinesthetic memories remembers body movements.
4. *"First reach agreement about which words you want to practice. Record them. Then decide which team member will time the event and keep track of the spelling. The other two group members will toss a ball back and forth. Each time the ball is tossed a letter is named. Keep the ball going back and forth until the word is spelled. Alternate roles so that everyone in your group has a chance to record, time and spell!"*
5. Distribute the materials to each group. Remind students about the expectations. *"You are to learn (practice, review) your spelling words."* Etc.
6. Monitor group's interactions. *"I hear Pat calling herself the Spell Checker. I like it!"*
7. Ask each group of three to share their results and discoveries. *"What was easy about using your body and kinesthetic memory to learn spelling words? Which way seems to work best for you?"*
8. *"What social skill did you perform effectively today?"*
9. *"Bravo! I saw everyone working together to learn their spelling words."*

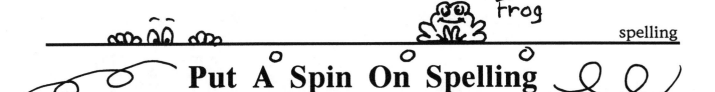

Put A Spin On Spelling

Imagine what it would be like if you could learn your spelling words painlessly. This activity will help you perk up your spelling ability and and you'll have fun doing it.

Directions

1. Record the words from your spelling list that are giving you trouble.
2. Take turns writing them with fun stuff.
3. Start the clock every time you write a word.
4. Record how long it takes you to write the word so that your partner can read it.
5. Take turns. Talk about this way of learning to study and spell words.
6. What happened? What thoughts do you have about time? How did you do? Are you surprised?

Star

Spelling Words	_____'s Time	_____'s Time

We used _____ to write our words! Artful!

In this activity, you used your kinesthetic memory. Your kinesthetic memory remembers a pattern of body movement. You also used your visual memory. It remembers what you see. Wild!

WOOSH

Speed Reading

This event is for those of you who like to take chances and experiment with new ideas. It will help you learn your spelling words. Participate! Cooperate! Have fun!

Directions

1. Record the words from your spelling list that are giving you trouble.
2. Use a magazine or a book. Look through it and find each word.
3. Start the timer!
4. Record how long it takes you to find each word. See what happens.
5. Take turns. Talk about this way of learning to study and spell words.
6. Why are some words easier to find than others? How did you do?

Spelling Words	_____'s Time	_____'s Time

Your eyes and your partner helped you in this job. You used your visual memory too. How does all this fit together with the words on your list?

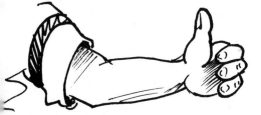

WAY TO GO!

Spelling is WOOF FUN!

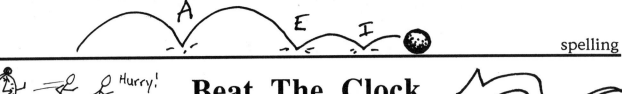

Beat The Clock

Do you like to play ball? If your answer is yes, then try this special event. It will help you learn your spelling words, too.

Directions

1. Record the words from your spelling list that are giving you problems.
2. Who will be the timer and spell checker? You have to keep track of your friends' spelling and the timer.
3. The idea is for you and another member of the team to toss a ball back and forth until a word is spelled- correctly. Each time the ball is tossed a letter is named by the tosser. Don't try to get fancy; just try to keep the ball in play.
4. If you misspell the word you have to start over. The clock keeps running.
5. Take turns so that everyone has a chance to toss and spell & time and check.
6. Talk about what you notice. Why do some words become a fast rally and others a slow one?

Spelling Words	Time (s)

_____, _____ and _____ worked together in an especially cooperative way! How's your time sense? How did you and your group members work together to learn?

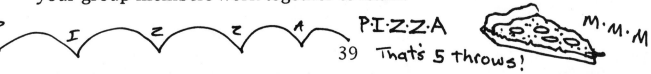

P·I·Z·Z·A   M·M·M

That's 5 throws!

Spelling For Two

As you may have noticed over the past several years, rank and file educators have become perceptibly more and more involved with and enthusiastic about whole language. As teachers continue to teach, take risks, model, and provide lots of opportunities for guided practice, spelling remains an issue. Inspired by the successes of our advisory board, we offer three knock-your-socks off strategies that are specifically directed to the whole language process. They can easily be used in conjunction with the previous games. All together, they're the best in the galaxy.

Statistics For Smart Spellers

Statistical Fun transforms the operation of discovering the rules and compiling a core word list into a good time spelling event. Another boon-it's interdisciplinary.

Materials
pencils
copies of the Statistical Spelling Fun reproducible
literature

Directions
* Our experts advocate using this activity as a follow-up to a mini-lesson in which you help children form generalizations about spelling rules. Explore sources of interesting words.
1. After you've taught a mini-lesson to help your students develop spelling rules (grapho-phonic generalizations, suffixes, prefixes, root words, etc.) invite your students to generate other words that fit the pattern and to analyze the results.
2. Divide your students into groups of two.

3. Review the rule, noting the exceptions. Have students suggest hypotheses about why some words violate the rule(s) and the spelling pattern(s). Use unabridged dictionaries to confirm students' hypotheses.

4. Introduce the task. *"Today we're going to discover more words that fit the pattern of ..... and have some statistical spelling fun. In your groups of two you will collect and think of many other words that fit our rule(s). Use our wall charts, our core list of words, the books in our library, print around the classroom, etc. You will keep a record like this."* Distribute the activity sheet.

5. Monitor each pair's progress. *"Why does that book have more words that the one John used, Linda? What do your results show so far?"*

6. Ask groups to share their findings. *"Why do you think fewer words end in ___sion than in ___tion? How many words from our science (social studies, etc.) lesson did you discover that fit the pattern? Do the exceptions outnumber the rule?"*

7. *"How did you share responsibilities? Did you divide the task? How?"*

8. *"Today I saw and heard..."* (summarize social and academic understandings).

Curiosity

Statistical Spelling Fun

Collecting the information for this activity will help you think about and remember spelling rules. This kind of information is called statistics. You're probably wondering what spelling has to do with statistics. Good! Curiosity about words is one of the important steps to becoming a writer.

Directions

1. Write the rule(s) or pattern(s) that you're learning.
2. Think of the words you know that fit the rule(s) or pattern(s). Look for more words in the classroom, in books and other places.
3. Keep a record of the words you find.
4. What does your chart show? What do you notice about these words? Talk about it. How can you explain the results?

The Rule or Pattern is _____

_____.

WORDS That Fit	WORDS That Should Fit But Don't (Exceptions)

This spelling information was collected and recorded by the cooperative pair of _____ & _____!

Give It A Go

Give It A Go helps encourage kids to be good spellers by taking the fear out of it. It's a little like riding a bicycle. *"You can do it if you give it a try, especially with a little help from a friend."*

Materials

pencils
copies of the Give It A Go reproducible

Directions

*This is an on-going activity that will become a vital part of your class routine.
1. Form pairs. Ask partners to talk about words. For example, *"What ambitious word did you learn last week?"*
2. Present the procedure. *"When we write we often come across words that we think are probably misspelled. Sometimes they are misspelled but many times they're spelled right."* Relate a personal experience. *"Today we're going to try a new way to learn our spelling words."*
3. Distribute the reproducible form.
4. Explain. *"When you finish a piece of writing, or an entry in you journal, etc., look it over for words that you think are misspelled. Write them down in the first column. Try to limit yourself to (five) words. Look at the words. Examine them. Be a word detective. Think about what you know about patterns and rules. Think about words that are like the words you've written. Then, give it a go and respell the word in the second column. At this point, find your partner and have a conference. What does he think? Talk about your ideas. Try to reach agreement. Play around with the words together. Then, rewrite it in the third column if you need to change a letter or letters."*
5. Model the process. Remind students to ask you or another adult for help or a conference when they are unsure of a spelling. *"Use your dictionaries!?* Etc.
6. Have students practice the routine. *"Surprise! You did know how to spell that word!"*
7. Implement group processing. *"How did you offer help to your partners? How will this help your writing?"* Etc.
8. Students should keep these sheets in their writing folders. Have new forms readily available.

A~B~C~D~E~F

Give It A Go

This is your chance to show how much you know about spelling! You'll probably surprise yourself with how much you know about spelling rules and patterns.

WORD	My First Try	My Second Try	Revised Version

Speller _____

Spelling Partner_____

Spelling Survey

This activity tops off our offering of spelling activities. (You probably are thinking that we've thrown everything but the kitchen sink at spelling.) Here's what you get- a collaborative activity that gets kids thinking about words, about the spelling process, communicating and that links language arts with math!

Materials

pencils
copies of the Spelling Survey reproducible

Directions

1. Introduce the activity. *"Today we're going to find out what you think about spelling. How do you feel about it? Do you think you're a good speller? Do you like to use your personal dictionaries? Do you use your visual memory to help you spell? These are some of the questions you are going to ask your classmates. The results will help us make more sense of spelling."*
2. Distribute the survey form. *"When you make a survey, you collect information. Who remembers what we call this kind of information? Right, it's statistics. Statistics are numerical pictures."* Discuss.
3. Inform students of and discuss the social skills they need to practice for this activity such as active listening, encouraging, etc.
3. Allow students time to circulate. *"This is your time to spiel. Tell what goes on in your head. Focus on your ideas."*
4. Circulate. Encourage. *"What are some reasons for the answers you're recording, Allan?"*
5. Compile the collected information in a class chart. Discuss the results. *"Why do you think more people learn how to spell from reading books than from other things they do? Do you think people would give you the same answers a month from now? Why? Did any answers surprise you? In what ways?"*
6. Implement group processing. *"What helped you work together as a large group? What made it easy for everyone to participate? Name one way you worked cooperatively."*
7. *"Today you..."* (summarize academic and social learning).

SPELLERS...
Talk about words
read, use books like dictionaries
listen to sounds
think about sounds
think about patterns
think about syllables
Go For It!!

Spelling Survey

When kids in Klutzville Elementary School were asked about their favorite books, one of the top four winners was personal dictionaries! Do you rank your personal dictionary as a winner? How about taking a survey to find out what your classmates think about spelling? See if the results surprise you.

Directions

1. Read over each question.
2. Make guesses. What do you think the responses will be to these questions.
3. Ask these questions to your classmates.
4. Think about the answers you got. Are you surprised? Talk it over.

Do You Like Spelling?	
YES	NO

Do You Think Spelling Is Important?	
YES	NO

Are You A Good Speller?	
YES	NO

WHICH MAKES SOMEONE A GOOD SPELLER?			
Reading	Making Lots of Mistakes	Practicing	Knowing The Rules & Patterns

WHAT HELPS YOU THE MOST WHEN YOU DON'T KNOW HOW TO SPELL A WORD?			
Wall Charts	My Personal Dictionary	Talking With My Partner	Sounding The Word Out

Chapter Three
Math, Cooperative
Games & Activities

Way back in the mathematical Stone Age (1992), we joined forces with the National Council of Teachers of Mathematics (NCTM) and came out with **Cooperative Learning, Math and Success.** It's still hot today. It expressed the consensus of research literature for the future direction of mathematics. It presented a cache of leading cooperative strategies with an adventurous spirit and a positive message. Small wonder that when you read this chapter, it's a cool experience. It too will expand your cooperative math power beyond your wildest dreams. Take advantage of the array of active, cooperative approaches to teaching and learning mathematics contained wherein. It will change the way you think about mathematics forever.

Hot Tickets
A new orientation for Mathematics!

• Take into account what the student can contribute to the learning
• Consider how your students intercept math concepts!
• Research shows that children actively construct and invent mathematical knowledge.

Quick Studies

When you take off from the starting line and begin teaching a new class, a new topic or present a new problem, don't you wonder about what your students are thinking, feeling, questioning and cogitating? Or why things start to go wrong? Beep. Not enough meaning making. Beep. Not enough emphasis on self-explanation. Beep. Not enough engagement in understanding performances. What can you do? Take a different approach. Quick Studies is all about accessing students' curiosities, attitudes and points of view. It will help them cement and extend their understanding of math by talking about it in groups of two. It uses the strategy of **Think, Pair, Share** (Lyman and McTighe 1988).

<u>Directions</u>

1. Form pairs.
2. Invite students to interact with each other. Pose a problem or ask them to generalize a concept, to take a stand, to support opinions, to elaborate or give them a question to answer.
3. Ask students to think about it. *"What makes sense to you? What do you already know about this? What connections can you make?"*
4. Wait 3-10 seconds. *"Take some time to think it over."*
5. Ask partners to explain it. *"Share your thinking and ideas with each other. Turn to your partner and talk. Explain your ideas. Take turns."*
7. Have partners communicate with the class. *"Let's talk about your ideas. Who wants to go first? Let's hear from others."* Etc.
8. Implement group processing. *"How did you and your partner use your experiences to answer this question? What did you do to explore each other's points of view?"*
9. Here's a saddlebag of ideas to get you started. They're all within your reach and can easily adapted to fit the needs/interests/learning styles of your class.

"Think about _____ and then share your idea(s), solution(s) answer(s), understanding(s) with your partner....."

* what math means to you.
* what makes sense to you about...probability, estimating, multiplication, graphing, surveying, etc.
* what you already know about.....
* why it's easier to learn math from each other as well as from me.
* one thing that we do in our math class that's cooperative.
* how you feel when we start an unfamiliar topic (or a new problem).
* one way you use math everyday.
* ways _____ is similar to _____.
* ways in which (multiplication) is different from _____.
* people who need to be math experts to do their jobs.
* what makes a person an expert in math.
* what a person has to do to become a math expert.
* a number that you might choose to represent who you are. Explain your choice.
* what it means to be mathematically-minded.
* whether or not you consider yourself to be a good mathematician. Explain why you think so.
* what you do when you don't understand what the problem is.
* what kind of math you like to do.
* how good problem solvers draw, visualize or use props to solve problems.
* how good problem solvers approach seemingly impossible problems in logical ways.
* how students with math power break out of their thinking ruts.
* how students with math power look for patterns.

10. These ideas can also be used for learning long prompts.

Views, Reviews & Previews

This activity uses the *"we can do it"* spirit of Team-Up (Kagan 1990) to foster positive interdependence and thinking-centered learning. The philosophy behind it: *"Know thy student"* (and his/her understanding of mathematics).

Materials

index cards
felt-tipped markers
glue
scissors

Directions

1. Make game cards. Reproduce the list of questions that follow or invent your own.
2. Divide your class into groups of four.
3. Students pair-off within their groups. Partners number off. *"One." "Two." "One." "Two."* Then, topic (#) 1 partners get together on one side of the room and topic (#) 2 partners on the other side.
4. Distribute the materials.
5. Present the task. *"Work together to solve the problems, answer the questions, etc. on the task cards. Use what you know. Talk about and identify strategies. Think about drawing, visualizing, using props, looking at simpler models and approaching the problems in logical ways. Be able to explain your thinking. When you have thought through the problems carefully and can demonstrate(explain, etc.) your understanding, return to your original group to share your discoveries."*

6. Teams reunite and partners **talk**.

7. Implement group processing. *"How were you able to reach agreement in your groups? What good problem solver strategies did you use? Did you need more information? What connections did you make with each other?"*

8. Examples of Views, Reviews & Preview questions:

* What makes (multiplication) easy?
* Name at least two ways numbers help us...interpret information, make decisions, solve problems, describe quantities. Give examples.
* Why aren't numbers just symbols?
* In a number, what power does the position of the digit have? (Offer an example.)
* In what ways are (addition) and (subtraction) related to each other?
* How do you know when to use (division)?
* What do you do when you (measure)?
* What do you have to think about when choosing a tool for measuring?
* What five patterns in mathematics can you name? Give examples.
* How can data (or information) be organized?
* In what ways does a collection of information (or data) help you make predictions?
* When is it helpful for you to analyze probabilities?
* What steps do you have to take to sort or classify objects?
* Why is it important to have some organizational skills in mathematics?
* What does math have to do with language arts (social studies, science, etc.)?
* Think of at least two things in math that go with these letters- C,S,T,P,L,I and W.
* Think of at least two pairs of number buddies.
* Why do you think some people can do math faster than others can?
* Think of at least two math questions about a (pencil).
* How big is big? Small is small? Etc. Give an example.
* Name two ways you've taken risks in problem solving.

9. Sharpen the excitement and add another dimension to this activity. <u>Time </u>the problem- based learning portion. *"You have two minutes to answer three of the five questions I've given you."*

Card Sharks

Try these games in your classroom and almost immediately you'll hear hails and hurrahs. (Optimism never hurts.) Card Sharks works in groups of two. It calls on the strategy of Corners (Kagan 1990) to introduce students to two fast, fun fact games. Students share the responsibility for learning math facts and must organize themselves to do it well.

Materials

at each Corner:	Corner II
* felt-tipped markers	* copies of the Cover Up reproducible
* index cards, tagboard or heavy construction paper	* counters (buttons, cubes, etc.)
* math fact sheets	
* stopwatches or timers	

Directions

1. Students need sheets that lists the math facts they are to practice. Determine what operations you want them to learn (review).
2. Prepare stations. Each station can be a cluster of desks or an available table. Identify each with a sign of the game that is to be played. Prepare the materials. Make a sign explaining the directions for each game. Game directions:

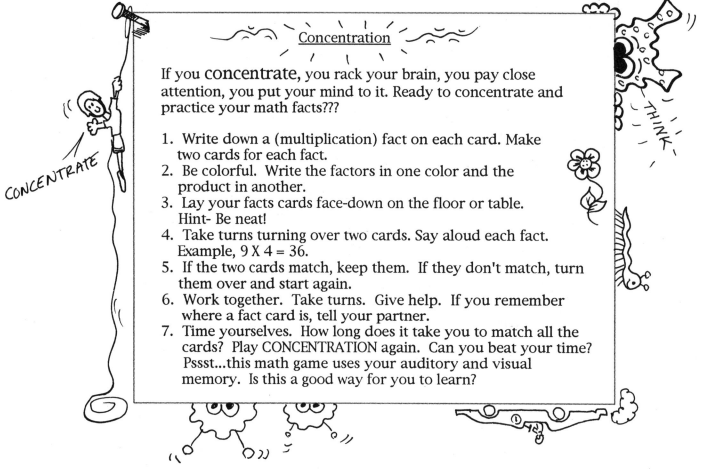

Concentration

If you **concentrate**, you rack your brain, you pay close attention, you put your mind to it. Ready to concentrate and practice your math facts???

1. Write down a (multiplication) fact on each card. Make two cards for each fact.
2. Be colorful. Write the factors in one color and the product in another.
3. Lay your facts cards face-down on the floor or table. Hint- Be neat!
4. Take turns turning over two cards. Say aloud each fact. Example, 9 X 4 = 36.
5. If the two cards match, keep them. If they don't match, turn them over and start again.
6. Work together. Take turns. Give help. If you remember where a fact card is, tell your partner.
7. Time yourselves. How long does it take you to match all the cards? Play CONCENTRATION again. Can you beat your time? Pssst...this math game uses your auditory and visual memory. Is this a good way for you to learn?

CONCENTRATE

THINK

3. Use the reproducible to list appropriate numbers that will appear as answers on the flashcards.

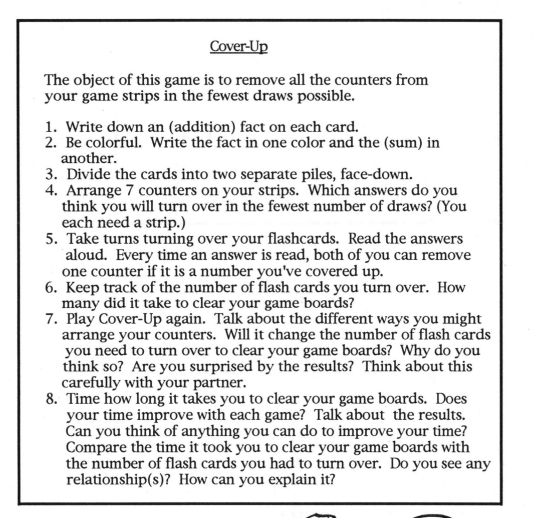

Cover-Up

The object of this game is to remove all the counters from your game strips in the fewest draws possible.

1. Write down an (addition) fact on each card.
2. Be colorful. Write the fact in one color and the (sum) in another.
3. Divide the cards into two separate piles, face-down.
4. Arrange 7 counters on your strips. Which answers do you think you will turn over in the fewest number of draws? (You each need a strip.)
5. Take turns turning over your flashcards. Read the answers aloud. Every time an answer is read, both of you can remove one counter if it is a number you've covered up.
6. Keep track of the number of flash cards you turn over. How many did it take to clear your game boards?
7. Play Cover-Up again. Talk about the different ways you might arrange your counters. Will it change the number of flash cards you need to turn over to clear your game boards? Why do you think so? Are you surprised by the results? Think about this carefully with your partner.
8. Time how long it takes you to clear your game boards. Does your time improve with each game? Talk about the results. Can you think of anything you can do to improve your time? Compare the time it took you to clear your game boards with the number of flash cards you had to turn over. Do you see any relationship(s)? How can you explain it?

Cover Up

$\sqrt{7+9}=$

$7+6=13$

$\boxed{2+8=10}$

$\boxed{4+7=11}$

$\boxed{8+5}=$

Your math life is about to be completely transformed. When you play this game you will practice your math facts, think about how likely (or unlikely) something is to happen and have an awesome time doing it.

Directions

1. Use this sheet to record the number of flash cards you had to turn over to clear the board and the time it took you to clear the board

2. Look over the numbers. Think about the math facts you're about to practice. Talk about it with your partner.

3. Choose 7 numbers. Arrange a counter on each.

4. Take turns turning over the flash cards you made. Read aloud the answers.

5. For every answer that is read, all players can remove a counter if it is on that particular number that is turned over.

6. Keep track of the number of flash cards you have to turn over to clear the board.

7. Time yourselves. How much time does it take to clear your board? What does the time have to do with the number of flash cards turned over?

8. Play this game again. Talk about the results. Be able to explain it.

How many flashcards will it take to clear the game board?	
GAME 1	GAME 2
How much time will it take to clear the gameboard?	
GAME 1	GAME 2

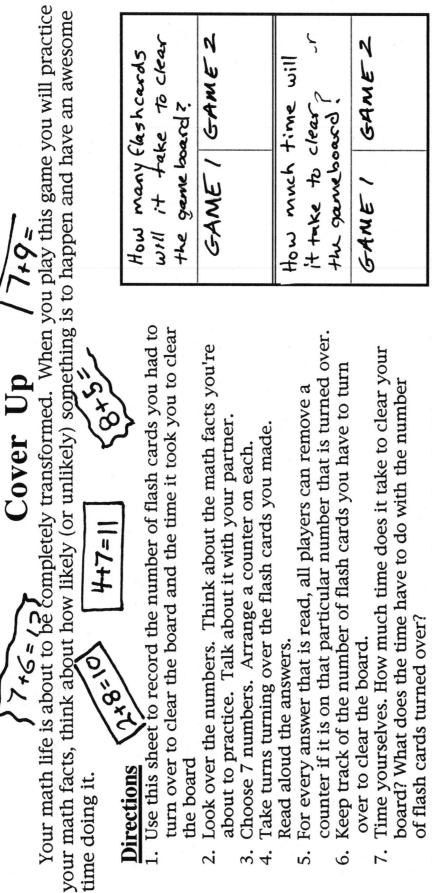

Prime Time

Got a second? A minute? Ready for an activity that will be time well spent? Prime Time will tickle your students' time zones. Wait a minute. Time out. It also gives kids a chance to estimate, think strategically and evaluate.

Materials
stopwatches or timers
copies of the Prime Time reproducible
pencils

In the nick of time ... once upon a time...

Directions
1. Divide your class into groups of four. Pair off students within each group.
2. Discuss the idea of time. *"How does time pop up in your life?"* Turn to your partners and share your ideas. *"Are you a clock watcher? Do you need to set the alarm to wake up on time in the morning? How long is a minute? What can you do well in a minute? Name an activity that takes five minutes."* Etc.

Think about your guesses in different ways. Be proud of a different idea!

3. Now for the Big Time. *"Today we're going to explore time. We're going to get a feel for time and your time talent."*
4. Distribute the materials.
5. *"First, read the questions at the top of each box. Then, estimate how long it will take you to do this activity. Record your guesses. Start the stopwatch when you begin the event. Stop it as soon as you are finished. Talk about the results. How close were your estimates? Were they way off? Why do you think so?"*

Time

- Good Morning -

My guess is 2 minutes!

6. You can assign roles for this activity:

Timekeeper- Is responsible for starting and stopping the stopwatch or timer.

Time Checker- Is responsible for recording.

7. Circulate and monitor groups' progress. *"What decisions are you making? What are you thinking about? Are you sharing ideas?"*

8. Ask partners to rejoin their groups of four to share what they learned. *"I thought this would be a fun way to practice time. Think about how we measure the passing of time. Did you approach each problem in a systematic or logical way? Were you surprised by the results? Did you get better at predicting? Why do you think so? What do you think would happen if you did each event again? Why? In what ways will this help you in the real world?"*

9. Implement group processing. *"What did you do to teach what you learned to the other members in your group? What did you do to share the information? Name one way you worked cooperatively."*

Our guesses were closer when we didn't have to think!

★ Prime Time ★

Time's Up! You are about to find your time talent in these two-person events of strategic thinking.

Directions

1. You'll need a pen or pencil and a stopwatch.
2. First, read the questions at the top of each box. What's the idea behind each event? How long do you think these things will take you to do? Compare each to the length of time you know it takes you to do something.
3. Estimate how long each event will take you to do. Record it.
4. Now, do the activities. For each event, start the stopwatch when you begin. Stop it as soon as you're finished.
5. Talk about the results. How close were your estimates? Were they way off? Close? Why do you think so? Do you have a better sense of a minute?
6. When would it be important to do one of these events faster?
7. Do these events again. Can you improve your times?

The Way Cool Events

a - b - c - d - How long does it take you to spell awesome backwards? Our estimate _____ Our time _____	How long does it take you to do fifteen jumping jacks? Our estimate _____ Our time _____
How long does it take you to name ten rivers? Hint- they can be anywhere in the world. Our estimate _____ Our time _____	How long does it take you to write your teacher's name? Each letter has to be a different color. Our estimate _____ Our time _____
How long does it take to sing "Three Blind Mice" alternating each word between you two partners? Our estimate _____ Our time _____	How long does it take you to draw each other from the shoulders up? The portraits have to be recognizable! Our estimate _____ Our time _____

Solid Foundations

Math activities, at least the really good ones, put the emphasis on *"using your bean."* They help students become flexible thinkers who are comfortable with what mathematics is ALL about and are able to apply mathematical ideas and skills to a range of problem solving experiences. Solid Foundations makes this happen as students build structures, visualize different geometric forms and begin to notice relationships. (You'll probably get the feeling that if you wanted to make the sky flash lightning, this activity could do that, too.)

Materials

cubes (wooden or mmmm...sugar)
containers
copies of the Solid Foundations reproducible

Directions

1. Divide your students into groups of four. Pair off students within each group. *"Think about what a cube is. Turn to your partner and explain your ideas."* Discuss.
2. Present the activity. *"Today we're going to become home builders. We're going to build cubes of different sizes."*
3. Distribute the containers of cubes.
4. You might want to assign roles:
   Foreman: Is responsible for the materials.
   Draftsman: Is responsible for recording.
5. Hold up 1 cube. *"How many sides (faces, edges...)?"* Explore students' ideas, then, draw a cube on the board that has 4 cubes on one side. *"Predict how many cubes it will take altogether to build a cube with 4 cubes on each side. Turn to your partner and discuss your guesses."*
6. *"We know that cubes have length, width and height, so we think that it will take 8 cubes all together."*
   "That will make 4 cubes on each side."
7. Have students build their cubes.
8. *"What happened? Were your predictions way off? How can you explain it?"* Encourage students to share their surprises and discoveries.
9. Distribute the reproducible. *"You will be building cubes of different sizes and recording the information on these charts. Think about what you understand from the cube we just built. Work together and share your ideas. Explain your thinking to your partners."* Etc.

10. Monitor groups' progress. *"What made you think of naming the cubes faces, Nancy?"*

11. Ask partners to return to their groups. *"Together, talk about what you learned. What conclusions can you reach? What kinds of patterns or relationships did you discover?"*

12. Record the information on a class chart to help children summarize the information they gathered. *"What strategies did you use? What did you do? Did you build models? How did it help you?"*

13. Implement group processing. *"How did you share the work? In what ways did you offer help? On a scale of 1-10 what would you give your group's cooperative performance for this task?"*

14. As an extension to this activity, ask students to work backwards. Have students build cubes of different sizes. Partners have to guess how many cubes were used and then determine the answer. Try asking students to build pyramids, rectangles, triangles and other shapes, too.

Solid Foundations

What does building have to do with mathematics? How can geometry help you appreciate the world in which you live? You deserve an explanation. The answers are here. Ready?

Directions

1. Build cubes of different sizes.
2. Predict how many cubes you need to use to build bigger cubes.
3. Use this chart to help you record the information.
4. Talk about the results.
   What surprises you? Why?
   Do you notice any patterns and relationships? Write about your findings.

How many cubes in all?	How many cubes is 1 side?
8	
27	
	12
	16
125	

We learned _____

_____

Signed,

_____

&

_____

Fractions Are Happenin'

They're not exactly a trend. Some teachers still shy away from fractions, but a strong <u>number</u> undercurrent is flowing through schools these days. For example, we use numbers everyday to interpret information, make decisions and solve problems. *"Is this a good price? Can I really afford these jeans?"* And thanks to the new NCTM standards, experiences in using number to determine or define quantities and relationships, to measure and to make comparisons are also making waves. Fractions Are Happenin' is emphasizes the idea of <u>whole</u>, a concept critical to any fraction lesson. It's a high-octane math activity during which students work in groups of three or four to find fractional parts of a whole and to write fractional numbers.

Materials

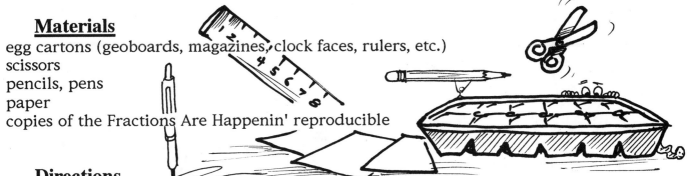

egg cartons (geoboards, magazines, clock faces, rulers, etc.)
scissors
pencils, pens
paper
copies of the Fractions Are Happenin' reproducible

Directions

*This activity assumes that students have had previous experiences with fractions.
1. Divide your students into groups of three (or four).
2. Distribute one paper and one pencil to each group.
3. Pose a questions such as, *"What is a fraction? List as many answers as you can think of."* Each group member writes an answer on the paper and then passes it to the next student in the group. Remind students to check the previous student's work before contributing. The paper should go around and around the table until many, varied answers have been recorded.
4. Have groups report their results. Make a big class wall chart.

Fractions

parts   fragments
sections   rearrangement
pieces   halves
groups
units   thirds

½

2/3

¼

5. Discuss the ideas elicited and the process. *"How did you elaborate on other kid's answers?"* Etc.

6. Distribute the egg cartons, reproducible and scissors.

7. *"How many ways do you think an egg carton can be cut into equal sections? Find all the possible ways. Think aloud as you consider where to cut the sections out. Talk about it. Keep a record of all the possibilities on the activity sheet."*

8. Circulate. Offer help. *"How could you write that down, Laura?"*

9. Have groups share their results. Discuss. *"Why do you think that you couldn't find a way to divide your cartons into 5 (7,8,9,10 or 11) equal sections?"*

10. More fun! Present your students with a challenge. *"Discover all the different ways to make a whole egg carton using the pieces that you cut out. Keep track of the ways you find."*

11. *"Which group would like to explain what you found out?" "Anyone else?"*

12. *"In what ways did you help each other? How did you reach agreement on how to record the results?" "You found three different ways to record. All three ways are correct. They all mean the same thing."* Etc. Flash... social and academic learning come together.

Fractions Are Happenin'

It's a good idea to get first-hand experience with fractions. You probably use fractions when you decide how to share a pizza with your friends. This activity will help you understand fractions. It will also help you learn how to estimate better.

Directions

1. Make a guess. How many ways do you think the egg cartons can be cut apart into equal sections?

We think the egg cartons can be cut into _____

equal sections because _____.
Now for the investigation.

2. Find all the possibilities. Record the results. Talk about ways to name the sections. Hint-use fractions.

3. Was your prediction right? Was it way off? Why do you think so?

4. Here's a challenge. Ready? Find as many different ways as you can to make whole egg cartons.

5. Keep track of the ways you find.

6. Talk about the results. Be able to explain it.

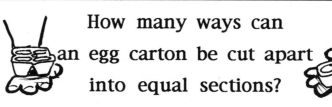

How many ways can an egg carton be cut apart into equal sections?

Sections	Number of cups	Fraction Name

Big Deal

This game is for the mathematically disinclined, for students who defy practice with addition, subtraction and multiplication of whole numbers. It pays homage to the idea that the recall of number facts is essential for real-life, for student confidence and for efficiency in developing broader numerical capability. WOW.

Materials

decks of playing cards
pencils
copies of the Big Deal reproducible
calculators

Directions

1. Take the face cards out of the decks. Each group of two needs one deck.
2. Divide your students into groups of three. Assign roles or have students self-assign:

   Dealer- The dealer deals the cards.

   Teller- The teller records the number facts in the correct columns.

   Checker- The checker checks the results with a calculator when a question arises.

3. Distribute the materials.
4. *"The object of this game is to add the playing cards that turn up and record the results. First, the dealer deals 2 (or 3) cards to each player including himself. Each player should (add) the numbers. Tellers record the sums on the Big Deal recording sheet. Keep playing until one number gets to the finish line. Reshuffle the cards when they've all been played."*
5. Circulate. Encourage groups to talk about the data they're collecting. *"I notice that you corrected this answer, Jim. What made you think that it might need checking?"*

6. Implement group processing. *"In what ways did the roles help you play Big Deal? How did you decide to check your answers?"*

7. Compile each group's results in a class chart. Discuss the results. *"Why do you think one sum wins more than others?"* Have groups play again. *"Do you think the results will be the same? Why do you think so? Share your ideas."*

8. Vary this activity. Have students practice subtraction or multiplication. Don't forget to make a new game recording sheet.

9. Walk on the wild side. a) Leave one of the picture cards in the decks. Call it a wild card. Let students assign it any number they wish. b) Leave all the picture cards in the decks. Continue the deck's number sequence. Let the Jack be worth 11 points, etc.

Big Deal

What's the big deal about practicing your math facts? You're about to find out...and have a good time.

Directions

1. You need a deck of playing cards, a calculator and a pencil.
2. The dealer deals 2 cards (unless your teacher tells you differently) to each player, including him or herself.
3. Each player adds the numbers that turn up.
4. Record the sums.
5. Keep playing! Don't stop until one number gets to the finish line.
6. If you need to, reshuffle the cards.
7. Use the calculator to check questionable answers.
8. Talk about the data you've collected. What do you notice? How can you explain it? Share your ideas.

Which sum will reach the finish line first?

4	5	6	7	8	9	10	11	12	13	14	15	16	17	18	19	20

Fini! _____ reached the finish line first. We think it "won" because _____ .

Signed, _____ , _____ & _____ .

About Face

Beyond question, probability is one area of mathematics that makes some of us queasy. The answer is, of course, to rethink our ideas about probability. Here is an activity that will make it a breeze. It will convince you and your students that probability is more than a hula-hoop kick...that the study of how often something happens is real- and fun. About Face is for groups of two or more players. It's mathspectacular.

Materials

decks of playing cards
pencils
copies of the About Face reproducible

Directions

1. Take out the jokers from each deck. Each group of (two) needs a deck of playing cards.
2. Divide your students into groups of (two). Assign roles or have students self-assign:
   Dealer- The dealer deals the cards.
   Teller- The teller records the results.
3. Distribute the cards, recording sheets and pencils.
4. Discuss the suits in a deck of playing cards. *"How many suits are in a deck of cards? What are the face cards in a deck? For each suit how many face cards are there? How many face cards in all? "* Etc. Groups should use the decks of cards to prove/disprove their answers.
5. Extra for experts- *"If you deal 13 cards face up, what is the chance that a Jack, Queen or King will turn up? How can you explain it?"*

6. "The object of this game is to record the face cards that turn up and record the results. First, the dealer deals 13 cards face up to each player, including himself. Count the number of Jacks, Kings and Queens. Then the tellers record the results. Do this at least 21 times."

7. Circulate. Encourage groups to talk about the data they're collecting. "How are you tallying your results? Why did you circle 13 under the column for the number of face cards, Ray?"

8. Implement group processing. "How did you divide the work? In what ways did the roles help? How did you share your thinking?"

9. Compile each group's results in a class chart. Discuss the findings. "How often should a face card turn up? What does our chart show? How can you explain it?"

10. Vary this activity. Follow the same process but use the About Face- II reproducible and....

   * Have students count and record either the Jack, Queen or
     King.
   * Have students count and record clubs, spades, diamonds or
     hearts.
   * Have students count and record red or black cards.

About Face

Significant inventions like CDs, major technological advances like the cellular phone and important scientific discoveries like penicillin all have at least one thing in common. Probability. In this activity you will experiment first-hand with probability.

Directions

1. You need a deck of playing cards and a pencil.
2. The dealer deals 13 cards to each player, including himself or herself.
3. Each player counts the number of Jacks, Queens and Kings.
4. Record the results.
5. Keep playing. Shuffle the cards and deal them at least 21 times.
6. Talk about the data you've collected. Write about what happens. What do you notice? How can you explain it?

How many face cards will turn up?

# of Tries	# of Jacks	# of Queens	# of Kings
1			
2			
3			
4			
5			
6			
7			
8			
9			
10			
11			
12			
13			
14			
15			
16			
17			
18			
19			
20			
21			

About Face II

Calling all card-carrying mathematicians. It's time to experiment with probability again.

Directions

1. You need a deck of playing cards and a pencil.
2. Fill in the missing information on the recording grid.
3. Now the directions get tricky. Read carefully.
   a. If you're experimenting with the probability of a Jack, Queen or King turning up, deal 3 cards.
   b. If you're experimenting with the probability of spades, diamonds, hearts or clubs turning up, deal 4 cards.
   c. If you want to see how likely a red or black card will turn up, deal 2 cards.
4. Keep playing. Shuffle the cards and deal them at least 21 times.
5. Talk about the data you've collected. Are you surprised? Why? What do you notice? Write about what happened.

How many face cards will turn up?

# of Tries	# of _____
1	
2	
3	
4	
5	
6	
7	
8	
9	
10	
11	
12	
13	
14	
15	
16	
17	
18	
19	
20	
21	

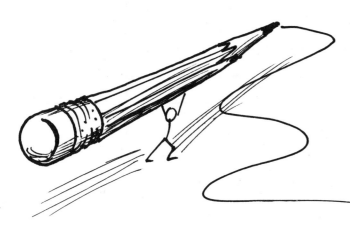

Diagonals Go Hollywood

Diagonals go Hollywood? Godzilla Meets Megashapes? Well, no, not exactly. But this math activity does go so far as to reinforce and facilitate children's own construction of numerical relationships as they share instructional materials and exchange ideas, explanations and information. We call it *interactive geometry applications.* (Whew!)

Materials

pattern blocks, Cuisenaire rods, cubes, blocks, paper cups, paper plates, recycled
    vegetable & meat trays & other manipulatives
rulers
colored pencils, felt-tipped markers
paper
copies of the Diagonals Go Hollywood reproducible

Directions

1. Form pairs. This activity can also be done in groups of three or more.
2. Draw a square on the chalkboard. *"A diagonal is a name for a line that connects opposite corners of shapes. How many diagonals does this square have? Take some time to think it over. Then, turn to your partner and explain your answer. Take turns."*
3. Discuss. *"What did you learn from each other's thinking?"*
4. Introduce the task. *"Today you and your partners are going to look for number patterns and relationships. Here's how...Take turns drawing different shapes. Make many, varied shapes with different numbers of sides. Use the manipulatives to help you create unique ones. For each shape, determine the number of diagonals. Keep track of the shapes and the number of diagonals that each shape has on the recording chart."*

5. Distribute the materials.

6. Circulate. Encourage students to be colorful. *"Maybe your group is thinking too much about drawing and counting. Try thinking about shapes in a different way, Celeste."*

7. *"As you collect the data, look for patterns. What relationships do you see? Explain your ideas to each other. Remember to look at different or simpler models."*

8. Ask groups to share what they learned. Make a big class chart to list their findings and ideas. Display the colorful results.

9. *"Can we find a second pattern from what we know?"* Etc.

10. Implement group processing. *"How did you share the work? Did you take turns?"*

11. *"Thinking about numbers when you're thinking about geometry could make you one of the smartest mathematicians in the business!"*

12. Make available compasses to older students.

13. Make a huge class graph of the information collected by your students.

Diagonals Go Hollywood

Mathematics is about to come to life. To make it happen, you are going to reinvent the shape of things. Engineer them. Experiment with them first-hand to discover number patterns and relationships.

Directions

1. Draw a shape. Be original!
2. Use the manipulatives to help you. Make them different colors.
3. How many diagonals does the shape have? Make a prediction. Explain your thinking to each other.
3. Draw diagonals by connecting the opposite corners of the shape.
4. How many diagonals does the shape have?
5. Record the number on the chart.
6. Create as many different shapes with many different sides as you can. Make predictions. Keep track of the results.
7. Now look for a number pattern in your chart. What relationship do you notice? How can you explain it?
8. How close were your predictions? Why do you think so?

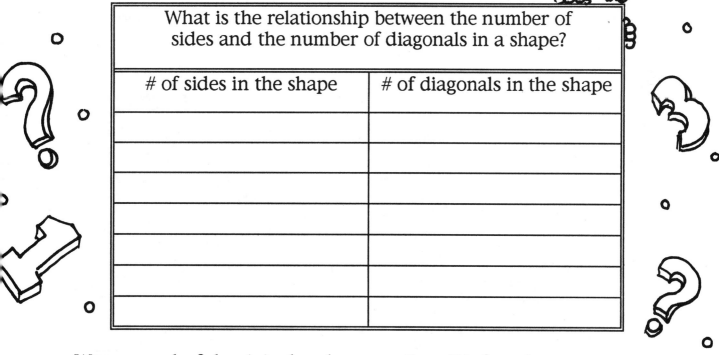

What is the relationship between the number of sides and the number of diagonals in a shape?	
# of sides in the shape	# of diagonals in the shape

We were colorful, original and cooperative. We found

_____.

Signed, _____ & _____

Wall Call

Here it is. Absolutely everything you need to integrate mathematics with science, language arts, social studies...That's how adaptable it is. Wall Call starts out with a ton of cooperative features for groups of four or more. But then, you can customize it, modify it or add to it. Planning a summer vacation should be so easy.

Materials

felt-tipped markers, colored pencils, crayons
Post-It Notes TM
reference materials
stopwatches or timers

Directions

1. Make a choice. What content do you want students to learn for understanding? Locate a myriad of resources. Engage students so that they have acquired meaning for the subject or concept and have made connections, sought new information, etc. Then, use Wall Call to build on their interest and give them experience with numbers, graphing and logic.

2. Organize your students into groups of four (or more).

3. Distribute the materials.

4. Introduce the task. *"Today you will create graphs to represent what you know about (butterflies). Here's how. First, draw as many different butterflies as you can in two minutes. Think about the butterflies we've read about, observed, etc. Use a different Post It for each butterfly you draw."*

5. Start the clock *now*.

6. When the time is up, have students decide how to organize their drawings. *"Share your butterfly drawings. Give information about each one. Talk about the color, the pattern, the wingspans, etc. Then work together to organize them. How can you arrange your Post Its? Reach agreement on how to sort and classify them. Everyone in your group should be able to explain the attributes and your system of classification."* Etc.

7. Have each group report. *"What generalizations can you share with us, Caroline? Why did your group choose different wing attributes?"*

8. Implement group processing. *"What was easy about sorting and classifying your drawings? How did you reach agreement?"*

9. Compile the drawings into a class graph. Ask each group to write three questions about it.

10. Learning log prompts will further students' understandings:

   a. How does a graph help you picture information?

   b. In what 3 ways do graphs help you compare facts?

   c. How can you explain the many, varied (butterflies) that were drawn? Write a sentence about it.

   d. What advice can you give someone about collecting data? Write at least two pieces of advice. Name at least 3 synonyms for graphing.

The Big Picture

Describe The Big Picture in a word...All right, how about four words? Challenging. Cooperative. Thinking-Centered. Active. The idea that there is no one way to think about any mathematical problem is not new. But sometimes you hit a pothole. *"No way. I can't approach the teaching of concepts of numbers differently."* Oh, yes you can. The Big Picture will involve students in a decidedly active role. It's a whole class lesson that provides students with experience in numbers, number facts and in discovering number patterns and relationships.

Materials
colored (washable) chalk

Directions
It helps to do this activity on a clear, sunny day. Some parental or adult help suggested.

1. To prepare, review the construction of a 0-99 chart with your class.
2. Tell students that they are about to go outside and construct a huge chart. *"...seeing number patterns is an important part of mathematics. It can help you learn your number facts and make sense of other problems. The purpose of The Big Picture is to look for number patterns and relationships. Be able to explain what you see."* Etc.
3. Next, go outside. Construct a chart from 0-the number of students in your class. Go on a pattern hunt as outlined in #4. Then, continue the chart to 50. Investigate the pattern that evolves. Last, continue the chart to 100. Students will anticipate the pattern-finding questions and discussion! Use the same color of chalk for each number sequence.

4. Pattern finding!!!! Ask questions that help the students with their search. Start with even numbers. Ask each student to find an even number and to stand on it. *"Take a look. What do you notice about where your classmates are standing? Do you see any patterns? Uncover the pattern you and your classmates have made. Break out of the paper and pencil thinking rut. What about the numbers you're standing on?* Etc. Now give each student a chalk of the same color. Have them circle all the even numbers. *"Be considerate of others. If someone else reaches a number you were going for, find another."* Discuss the patterns that emerge. *"What happens to the numbers as they go from left to right in each row? What if you look in the opposite direction? What if you look at the numbers in the columns? Diagonals?"* Etc.

5. Do the same for odd numbers. *"Draw squares around the odd numbers. What pattern(s) can you find? What happens to the numbers as you look in different directions? Make observations."* Draw a diagonal line from one corner to another to help students look for doubles. Guide them to look for other patterns... *"X the numbers that have 5." "Shade the numbers with digits that add to 7..."* Etc.

7. Discuss. Wonder. Speculate. *"How is (one) pattern like another? Is there a row, column, or diagonal that gets larger or smaller faster than the row or column next to it? What happens if you look for patterns in lines that are not straight up or down or diagonals? What do you notice about all the numbers that end in zero? How did you look for relationships? What reasons can you think of for the same pattern emerging? Did you make any predictions?"* Etc.

8. Implement group processing.

* Students might benefit from individual copies of the 0-99 chart for reference.

Facts of Math Chart

Seen in Missouri. And on the Million Dollar Mile near Boston. And in Missoula. Colorful, fascinating number charts that address recent research on the nature and development of children's mathematical understandings. How can the experiences of creating number charts, discovering patterns & relationships in number charts, and viewing number charts as interesting problems lead to an understanding of mathematics that makes sense, that seems natural, that works and that connects with what children already know as well as the abstract? The answer is best illustrated by trying one of our all-time favorite activities, Facts of Math Chart. Not bad for encouraging cooperation, either. Or, for helping you rethink mathematics and your role in teaching it.

Materials

large sheets of tagboard, poster board
felt-tipped markers, crayons
copies of the Facts of Math reproducible
copies of the 100 chart reproducible (optional)

Directions

*This activity gives students practice with multiplication facts. Because re-invention never stops in a classroom, you'll be able to adapt it easily to other operations.

1. Divide your class into groups of four.

2. *"It's time to develop math power. What does it mean to have math power? Think about it and turn to your group and share your ideas."*

3. Have a class discussion about students' ideas. Elicit statements about patterns. *"Looking at numbers that you can see helps you figure out what numbers are missing."* Make a class list.

4. "The object of this activity is to create a 100 chart and then uncover number patterns and relationships in multiples of 2,3, 4 and so on."

5. Distribute the chart paper and markers.

6. "Here's how. First, make a 100 chart of one color. Your numbers should be legible and easy-to-read. Once the chart is completed you will identify multiples of 2, 3, 4, 5 (etc.) using different colors and shapes. Get ready to make math power happen..."

7. Monitor groups. Have members give suggestions for improvement. Encourage them to share the work. Students might present their products.

8. "What do you know about multiplication? What patterns can you see as you look down the columns? Can you see any patterns across the rows? Are the patterns the same or different? How do patterns help you predict?"

9. Then, introduce the reproducible. Give directions for identifying other multiples if appropriate. "Talk about what comes next. Decide how to make a key for your chart. Knowing what to do and what comes next will help you take control of this task." Etc.

10. Facilitate the activity. *"What patterns are you discovering? Why do the patterns work? How does one pattern help you find another? How can you explain it? Why do you think this pattern is emerging? What do we know about even numbers? What do you remember from The Big Picture activity?"*

11. After students have thought through their explorations carefully, ask them to demonstrate their understandings. *"What group would like to present what they discovered first?"*

12. Focus the discussion on the number patterns and numerical relationships. *"Why do you think the multiples of 2 turned up in so many other patterns? In what ways did you knowledge of multiplication help? What is the relationship between the patterns of 5 and the patterns of 10? How is the ___pattern like the _____ pattern? In what ways are they different?"*

13. *"Congratulations. You understand the idea behind multiplication (repeated addition). You can explain different number patterns and apply what you know to number chart problems. Wow! Math power."*

14. Implement group processing. *"How did working in a group help you learn with understanding? How did working together help you think about number patterns more carefully? What did you do to cooperate?"*

15. Make a class display of students' 100 charts.

The Facts of Math

When you look at a 100 chart, you're getting a peek into a system that makes sense, that has lots of interesting problems and that can help you learn the number facts and have a swell time doing it. It's like searching for treasure that you know is there, if you can just find it.

Directions

1. Make a huge 100 chart. The numbers should be neat and legible. Use one color for all the numbers.
2. Don't forget to give it a title.
3. Now its time to unearth the treasure lurking there.
    * Circle all the multiples of 2.
    * Box all the multiples of 3.
    * Underline all the multiples of 4.
    * X all the multiples of 5.
    *
    *
    *
    *
    *
4. For each multiple, choose a different color.
5. Make a key that explains the colors and symbols you used.
6. Math Power-Talk about the patterns and relationships that you discover.
    +What do you notice?
    +How can you explain it?
    +Are any patterns the same?
    +In what ways are some patterns different?
    Clue- Notice the patterns in the rows, columns and diagonals.
7. Write about what you learned.

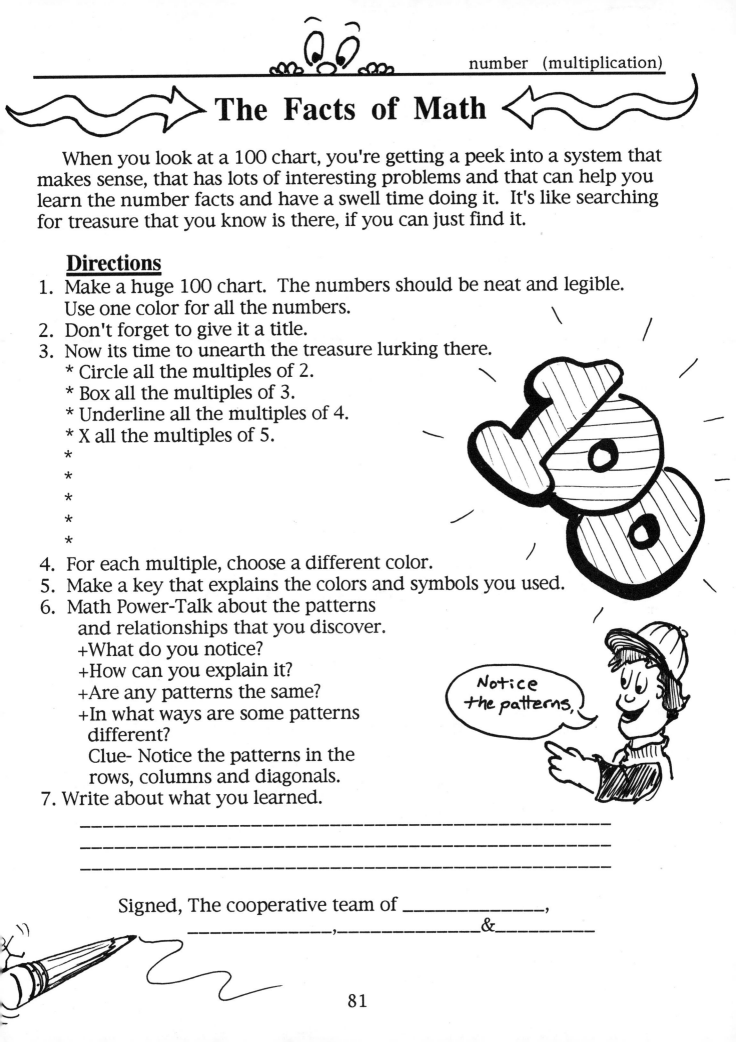

Notice the patterns,

_____
_____
_____

Signed, The cooperative team of _____,
_____,_____&_____

81

100 Chart

1	2	3	4	5	6	7	8	9	10
11	12	13	14	15	16	17	18	19	20
21	22	23	24	25	26	27	28	29	30
31	32	33	34	35	36	37	38	39	40
41	42	43	44	45	46	47	48	49	50
51	52	53	54	55	56	57	58	59	60
61	62	63	64	65	66	67	68	69	70
71	72	73	74	75	76	77	78	79	80
81	82	83	84	85	86	87	88	89	90
91	92	93	94	95	96	97	98	99	100

Chapter Four
Social Studies, Cooperative
Games & Activities

Once upon a time, you could position a map or a globe in your classroom, plot places from news articles and call it geography. You could create timelines, make applesauce and recite heroic speeches and, if all went well, ta-da, social studies was covered. But, in this area of change, what if you need to adjust your curriculum? What if you need to address the content standards identified by the National Council for the Social Studies and other educators as well? What if you need to provide for the study of continuity and change? Or community? Or cultural diversity? This new kind of social studies is cause for celebration. But it's also a challenge. The ideas for activities and games that follow will help you shift adeptly from the old goals to the new. From one corner of the world to another. You won't have to go any further to hear kids hip-hopping to the salsa beat or to eat a melting pot pizza. It's a cause celebre that keeps producing.

Melting Pot Pizza

It's more important than ever to explore multicultural connections with your students. Just think- in the last ten years, more people immigrated to this country since 1910. Melting Pot Pizza will help students appreciate diversity and deliver tantalizing aromas and much-anticipated flavors. It's a whole class *cooperative, interdisciplinary* activity that will result in a grand feast. Guaranteed delicious.

Ingredients

base your pizza toppings on special ingredients that come from the different
   cultural backgrounds of your students
fresh pizza dough (found in most supermarkets) or... you can use the recipe
   provided here or...you can buy focaccia, the rustic flat bread of Etruscan origin
   that predates the Neopolitan pizza by centuries or...you can use refrigerated
   biscuit or roll dough
aprons
utensils including pizza stones or cookie sheets, measuring spoons, measuring
   cups, timers, wooden boards, rolling pins (optional)
containers for the various ingredients
heat source for baking (*Preheat to 400 degrees)
clean-up supplies
copies of the Melting Pot Pizza reproducible (copy back-to-back)
copies of the Planet Wide Survey reproducible (optional)

Directions

* Adult and/or parent help suggested.
1. Immerse your students in the theme of ethnic diversity. Display artifacts. Post photographs, posters and portraits. Be BIG on multicultural literature. Read picture books with strong text and artwork, fiction, poetry, well-documented biographies, informational books and traditional works.
2. Meanwhile, get ready to stretch a little. Experiment and take chances. Decide on your pizza dough of choice.
3. Introduce this cross-cultural activity. *"We're about to venture into relatively unknown territory and make a melting pot pizza. Yummers! Who loves French fries? Who sometimes eats hamburgers? Turn to the person sitting next to you and share the name of one food that you know came from another country."*

4. Discuss. You might want the class discussion to lead to a discussion of the age-old, evolutionary process of culinary exchanges. *"Often through migration or conquest, new and unfamiliar foods were introduced into countries and then adapted and incorporated."* Etc.

5. *"Where did your family come from before they settled here? What special foods do you have? Let's think of many foods and spices."* List the foods and so on of your students' ethnic backgrounds. Determine which ones would be appropriate for pizza toppings.

6. Ask students to collect and bring in foods- the foods that will remind them of their connections to other people and places. Have a class discussion about the particular country or region from which the ingredients came. Make a chart.

* Check out the extension ideas for interdisciplinary connections that follow!

7. Organize six stations. (In a class of 24 students, 4 students can work at one station.) Each station can be a cluster of desks, a counter or an available table. Make available the necessary equipment at each.

8. Divide your class into groups of four. Each group will make one pizza. Read the instructions, explain the process, establish the rules and take your students on a tour of one station. *"Each group will cook (as independently as possible). You are the head chefs. The grown-ups are your assistant chefs. They will be at the stations to help. You and the members in your groups are responsible for learning with each other. You are expected to talk about the task and share the work."* Etc.

9. Remind students that these pizzas, although the ingredients are true to their traditional sources, will be original creations of their own.

10. Have a juke (from the Senegalese, meaning to have a wild time). The recipe is easy to follow, whether you make the pizza dough from scratch or choose another route.

11. *"Ready to eat the pizzas?"* No one will resist.

12. Debrief what and how students learned. As a way of reinforcing the belief that students are responsible for their own learning, have them evaluate their social skills. *"What difficulties did you experience in cooking together? How did you work them out? What did you do to help your group make pizza?"* Etc.

13. Put learning logs to work. Here are some prompts to adapt to your needs:
   a. What did you learn about the connections you have with other countries?
   b. In what 2 ways did this activity help make the world seem more close up and personal?
   c. How is food a global connection? Name at least 2 ways.
   d. Map or web your connections to another country or region in the world.
   e. What interesting discovery did you make about_____? Write 2 or 3 sentences about it?
   f. What connections do the foods of ___have with the geography of that country?

14. Cooking in the classroom will help everyone find, know and delight in <u>content connections</u>. High up on the interdisciplinary list are related **social studies** experiences:
   * Use stickers to identify the countries or regions from which the ingredients came on a map or a globe. You might also have children make small drawings of the foods they found to secure to a map or globe. Have a class discussion about the arrangements that result.
   * Kids will be positively energized by researching the cultural backgrounds of schoolmates. Use the Planet Wide Survey reproducible to help students organize their efforts. Seek the cooperation of your colleagues. After students collect the information, ask them to create mural-size graphs that illustrate their findings.
   * Straight Talk. Have students correspond with pen pals.
   Resources: Student Letter Exchange, 630 Third Avenue, NY, NY 10017- 212/557-3312 or World Pen Pals, 1690 Como Avenue, St. Paul, MN 55108.

If you've demonstrated a fearless acceptance of the good things in teaching that help kids discover connections or construct and expand their understandings of a topic, then here comes a trip to bountiful. Think **MATHEMATICS.**

* Investigate the Planet Wide Survey graphs made by your students. Have groups write at least 3 questions about their graphs for other groups to answer.

* The Name Game. Use the information collected from the Planet Wide Survey to have children make comparisons. Invite them to investigate questions such as: What country has the longest name? What country has the shortest name? What is the most common first letter in the countries' names? Which letter occurs most frequently in the countrys' names? Have students make a graph depicting their findings.

* Ask students to make a survey to investigate the different foods favored (or unfavored) by their classmates.

* Have students plan a trip to the country or region from which their family came. Encourage students to include critical factors such as means of transportation, mileage to and from their destination, traveling time, language spoken, currency, changes in time, type of clothing needed, interesting places to visit, accessibility, the natural environment and so on.

Melting Pot Pizza

Here's one of the most de-licious, most messy and most fun activities you will ever do in school. You'll love making this pizza as much as eating it. Melting Pot pizza celebrates the people of the world. Join together and have a juke! It's going to taste yummy!

Melting Pot Pizza! Recipe
(MAKES 1 PIZZA)

It's pizza time dudes!

Ingredients

1 recipe Schoolmade Dough or
    8 refrigerator rolls or biscuits
international toppings

Directions

1. Make or prepare the dough.
2. Have fun kneading and rolling out the dough. Get into the process. Make it any thickness you want.
3. Sprinkle the baking sheet or pizza stone with a little magic dust (a.k.a. cornmeal).
4. Put the pizza on it.
5. Brush the pizza top with olive oil.
6. Venture into topping territory. Talk about the countries from which they came. Have fun! Notice the colors, the smells, the shapes, the textures of these international toppings. Arrange them over the dough.
7. Bake about 15 minutes. The pizza should be brown around the edges.
8. Let it cool a little.
9. Mangia! Bon Appetit!

Creative Eating is our motto!

Schoolmade Dough

1 package of dry yeast
1 1/4 cups of lukewarm water
3 cups of unbleached flour
1 teaspoon of salt
1 tablespoon of olive oil

Squeeze!

Plunk!
Twist!
Punch!
Turn!

1. In a large bowl dissolve the yeast in 1/2 cup of water. Let it proof for 10 minutes.
2. Add the flour, salt, olive oil and remaining water. Mix well and knead until the dough is smooth, about 10 minutes. Add more flour if necessary to make it really smooth.
3. Put the dough in an oiled bowl. Cover with a cloth and let it 'rest' for about an hour. It should double in bulk.
4. Punch it down and let it 'rest' for another 10 minutes.
5. Roll the dough into a big, flat circle.

Calling all cooks. Did you use lots of cooperative skills to make this Okonomiyaki (Japanese for pizza)??? Did you share the work? Write about it.

_____

_____

_____

Now it's time to tell what you thought of the pizza. Give it a review!

_____

_____

_____

Signed, _____,_____

_____&_____

Yum!

Planet Wide

A survey is a way to collect information. It gets people talking. One person asks questions and the other person answers the questions. Planet Wide will help you investigate the cultural backgrounds of the kids in your school. You'll learn about other countries and the people who live there. Expand your horizons. You never know where you're going to end up and what you'll need to know.

Ask at least 10 classmates questions like these:

Where were you born?	
Classmate's Name	Name of Country

Where did your family come from before they settled here?	
Classmate's Name	Name of Country

What special _____ do you have? (foods, holidays, it's your choice!)	
Classmate's Name	Name of Country

Do you wear special things that belong to your cultural group?	
Classmate's Name	Name of Country

Save The Earth

Save The Earth recognizes one fundamental kid fact: playing is a natural way to learn. Whether they are negotiating a game of Earth Toss or making mud pies, it gets them acting, reacting, feeling, talking, and experiencing. So, take one large rubber (or vinyl) earth ball. Wait for sunny skies. Now go outside with your class. Let cooperative, social studies fun happen.

Materials
an earth ball

Directions

1. Have your students lie on their backs in a circle. Their heads should be toward the center. *"This is the epicenter!"*

2. Pose a question that encourages construction of imagistic associations, that links to other events, names, dates, etc. and/or recall of significant facts. Ex. *"Think of the many bodies of water found in the United States (or Canada, etc.)."*

3. The object of the game is for students to roll the earth ball around the circle using their arms to move it. Each time the ball is passed to a player, he must offer a response to your question. Encourage students to visualize. *"You're in the middle of Lake Superior. What is it like?"* Etc.

4. When a player is unable to come up with an answer, classmates can 'save the earth' by offering help.

5. Let your class suggest problems for this event.

6. Implement group processing. "What did you do to keep the ball rolling? Did you 'save the earth?' How did it feel? Did you receive help? How did it feel?" Etc.

Earth Toss

This is the game to use when your class needs some fact-paced, high-energy fun. Don't worry. The social studies connection is well-emphasized. It's brainstorming with a 'catch.'

Materials
rubber earth balls
stopwatches or timers

Directions
* Prepare a list of questions that focuses on the topic you want students to learn. Each question should have many answers.
1. Form groups of three.
2. Two students will toss the ball. The other group member will keep track of the number of answers given and the time.
3. Players stand facing each other.
4. The object of the game is to throw the ball back and forth without dropping it while naming many...kinds of communities, rights or responsibilities of a citizen, the physical features of your community, the human -made features of your community, reasons for rules, important attributes of leaders, factors influencing the growth or decline in population of a community, global links, etc.in (2) minutes.
5. Have students play several times. Switch roles so that everyone has a chance to keep track of the time and toss the ball.
6. *"How did it go? How did your partner's answers help you think of river names? Did (2) minutes seem like a long time? In what way did keeping track of the time help? What did you like?"*

Trailblazers

An activity with a sense of fun. An activity that entertains and engages young social scientists-to-be like none before it. An activity for groups of four or more. An activity that brings 'performance' assessment into your classroom. An activity that requires students to think and to put it all together in the form of an obstacle course of challenging events. An activity that makes you smile every time you use it.

Materials

a variety of fun stuff: cardboard boxes, string, fabric scraps, crepe
  paper, ribbon, yarn, string, paper scraps
tempera paint, felt-tipped markers, crayons
paint containers
paint brushes
old maps, newspapers and magazines
reference materials
scissors
copies of the Trailblazers Planning Sheet reproducible (copy back to
  back)

Directions

*Determine a large space where students can create and make their way through an obstacle course. Think about spaces, indoors or outdoors, that contain interesting features such as trees, walls, and so on that can be integrated into the obstacle course. Separate the area into smaller sections so that each group is responsible for one part of the obstacle course.

*Flexibility in scheduling is an important element to the success of this activity. At times, you might have to modify your expectations, strategies and role. But, be ready to explore uncharted territory and feel invigorated.

1. Organize your class into groups of four. (We're dividing the topic of immigration into six subtopics; hence, we're dividing a class of 24 students into groups of four.)

2. Introduce the activity. *"Today, we're going to transform an ordinary sit-in-your-chair-at-your-desk activity, into a beyond-your-wildest-dreams event. Colossal! We're going to build an obstacle course of events that will challenge us to demonstrate what we know about immigration. The obstacle course will be divided into six parts. Each group will be responsible for building a part of the course. The theme of this course will be immigration."*

3. Define the subtopics for each part of the course. Have a class discussion about immigration. *"You know a lot about immigration. We've...Now it's time to demonstrate and celebrate what you know. By creating and making your way through the course, you will think about decisions families immigrating to North America had to make, immigration routes and means of travel, words that have been borrowed from other languages, difficulties faced by immigrants who did not speak English, important places in our community that immigrants need to know about and etc."* Assign groups to subtopics or ask groups to choose a subtopic.
4. Distribute copies of the Trailblazer Obstacle Course Planning Sheet. Ask students to discuss it in their groups of four. *"How will it help you organize your task?"* Review what an obstacle course is. Discuss why this project format will be an intellectual as well as physical happening. *"Many obstacle courses are designed to test strength, how well a person can solve a problem, etc."* Have students share obstacle courses they've experienced. Discuss evaluation. *"This is what you will be graded on-"* Remind students that the product is important but that *"so is the way you work as a team."* Etc.
5. Make available art and building materials. Check out PVC pipe building systems.

6. Plan further experiences to help students. What skills are needed to help children meet the specified outcome? What instruction will help them rehearse the task?

7. Meet with groups. Discuss what sort of obstacles might be created at each section of the course. *"What tasks can you think of that will be fun and safe? What kinds of challenges can you set up that will ask your classmates to show what they know about.... "* Make lists of students ideas. Offer ideas. Younger children may need explicit directions. Write out directions for each station. Ex.

Often when a person immigrated to our country, he or she could not speak English. In order to communicate, he/she might have used motions rather than words to communicate. Do you think this would have been hard? Easy? Try it and see! Create a game of charades for your classmates to play. Make a list of 20 words for students to act out. Write them on pieces of paper. Animals, vegetables and other foods are good examples.

8. Allot an appropriate amount of time for each group to plan and create their course. Hold several class meetings so that students can share their progress, surprises, frustrations and enthusiasm. *"How are you sharing the work? Who can explain the steps you're taking?"*

9. Build the course. Have each group contribute their section.

10. Have adult and/or parent volunteers ready to help at each part of the course as children experience the Obstacle Course! Rotate groups of students through each section. Make it a happening!

11. Debrief what and how students learned. *"What difficulties did you experience? How did you work them out?"* Compare and contrast the tasks found at each station.

12. *"Colossal! Your obstacle course is artful and interesting. You met the challenges at each section!"*

Trailblazers Obstacle Course Planning Sheet
A Challenging Collection of Ideas

What makes a good obstacle course? In this case, challenging do-it-yourself activities that make you think with what you know. You can't really learn something unless you do something with it or make connections to it. For this project, you will work in a group to create a section of an obstacle course. The section will challenge them to use their skills, ideas and knowledge.

I will help my group create and build a section of an obstacle course. The topic is _____.

Directions

In order for you to build a part of the course, you'll need to search for and find supplies and materials that help test your classmates' knowledge and ability. Enjoy the hunt!

* old magazines and newspapers
* photographs
* music & sound effect tapes
* money
* maps
* flags
* other good hands-on stuff

Now it's time to get creative. Talk about the kind of obstacles you might build. What task will be fun? What will help your classmates show what they know about your group's topic? Get them analyzing, composing, performing, inventing, deciding, pretending, sorting, building, proving, experimenting, making.
Get them spinning a spinner, plotting a trip, playing a game, moving to music...Here are some ideas. Customize them. Have your classmates...

+ Make a collage about...in 5 minutes while singing or dancing to...
+ Make a Who's On The Most Wanted List about... and then do 40 jumping jacks alternating each one between members of the group.

+ Find their way through a mega maze that goes from....to ......
  by answering 5 questions about the topic correctly
+ Crawl through a tunnel after answering 3 tough questions
  about the topic...
+ Climb a mountain by identifying significant objects placed
  at 6 rescue (or rest) stations
+ Dress-up as very important people and hold a debate...a press
  conference...a talk show about the topic (You provide the
  props,your classmates provide the information- right?)
+ Interpret replications of art and artifacts or replications of
  primary source documents while whistling ...
+ Review or critique a computer-generated display while
  switching shoelaces and re-tieing them both

Your section of the obstacle course should feature:
* a plaque that explains the challenge
* labels or signs that give directions and tell the challenged what
  to do
* a variety of resources and interesting hands-on stuff

All Together Now- Your section of the Trailblazer Obstacle Course will
be evaluated on ...
  1) how well you 'tested' your classmates knowledge on the topic
  2) how interesting and unique the obstacle is
  3) how well you worked with your group
  4) the accuracy of the information presented and tested in the
      obstacle

Get Lost

Practice. That's what we're talking about here. The practice your students need in using maps and globes and in describing and locating places relative to other places. Get Lost will build on children's interest in navigation. It's an activity for groups of two or four.

Materials

maps and globes
Post-it Notes TM
pencils

Directions

1. Divide your class into groups of four.
2. Students pair off within their groups. Each partner pair is a navigational team.
3. Distribute the materials. Each group needs a map, a sheet of Post-it note paper and a pencil.
4. *"The object of this game is to find your lost classmates. First, one pair decides where to get lost. They will give clues to the other players, one at a time. Here's a catch- a clue cannot be repeated. Listen carefully. The search party guesses where the other team members are lost by using the information in the clues."*
5. Explain the way in which you want clues given- absolute location, relative location, names of specific places, etc.
6. *"Cut or tear the Post-it note into 2 small pieces. Partners, write your initials on the pieces. These will be your map markers."*
7. *"The other pair is the search party. You will work together to guess where your lost classmates are. Discuss, analyze and evaluate the clues given to you."*
8. Have teams switch roles so that everyone has a chance to be lost and to be part of the search party.
9. Implement group processing. *"What did you do to share the clues? What did you do to listen? Which type of clues were the most helpful? How can you explain this?"*
10. Provide for assessment.
11. *Have teams keep track of the number of clues given per turn.
Have them make a graph. *"What does your graph show? Did you get better at figuring out clues?"*Etc.

Before & After

Earthquakes. Floods. Volcanic Eruptions. Forest fires. Colossal oil spills. Nuclear accidents. Global crises that often affect a large segment of the earth's population, influence large areas of the earth's surface and require the cooperation of the world community to solve or improve. Before & After gives students, in groups of two or more, practice with location, the concept of change, and experience with thinking causally.

Materials

maps & globes
appropriate props
old magazines, newspapers, books
paper
colored pencils, felt-tipped markers, crayons
copies of the Before & After planning sheet reproducible

Directions

1. After engaging students in the theme of global crises, change or geology superstars, hold a classroom discussion to introduce the activity. *"You know a lot about different events that affect the earth."* Identify all the events or issues that may be considered global crises and/or with which children are familiar.
2. Divide your students into groups of three. Ask them to select one event that interests them. *"Is there one crisis that you are connected to in some way?"* Etc.
3. Assign roles:
   Project Manager- Leads the discussions and sees that all requirements are met.
   Presenter- Organizes the presentation to the class.
   Architect- Determines whether or not the items found are correct. Assists everyone in the search.
4. Explain the task. *"In your groups of three, you are going to research a global crisis and then teach others what you've learned."*
5. Distribute the activity sheet. Read and discuss the list. Make sure that everyone understands his/her role and the ways in which they will be evaluated.

6. Monitor groups' progress. *"I'm struck by how well all the members of Jane's group are contributing."*

7. Have teams present their projects. *"In what ways was the Mount St. Helens explosion a global crisis? Pat's group will now convince us that the Loma Prieta quake was a global crisis."* Etc.

8. Implement group processing. *"What was the most difficult part of this project? How did you solve the problem? What steps did you take? In what ways did the roles help?"*

9. *"You expanded your horizons and learned about how an event thousands of miles away can affect us right here in River City."*

Before & After

How does a global event thousands of miles away affect you? How does it affect the earth's surface?

You can find the answers to these questions and more by embarking on this hunt. There's a lot of colliding, exploding, crashing down and erupting going on out there. The more you learn about global crises, the more you can understand the influences it has on your daily life (and maybe work to do something about it)!

My group and I will become experts on the global crisis

_____.

Project- How were people and the earth affected by. . .

_____.

Directions

1. Locate the event.
2. Describe its location. Use a map or a globe to help locate the crisis. Write about it. Describe the place relative to other places. To what is it near?
3. What other places were involved?
4. How was the population of the place influenced? Try to discover at least one positive and three negative outcomes of the crisis.
5. Could this crisis have been avoided? What do you think? What ideas can you offer? Upon what are you basing your opinion?
6. Here's where you get to be creative. Think of a project format to share what you learned about the crisis. Here are some ideas. Find one that catches your interest and talent.
   * Stage a reenactment of the event.
   * Change history. Act out the event that didn't happen.
   * Produce a live "You Were There" show .
   * Retell the drama of the crisis as a play or news show.
   * Create a museum display of the crisis. Illustrate the happenings with flip, before and after pictures.
   * Create a computer-generated display. Include maps and graphs.

WOOSH

7. Each member of your group will be responsible for brain-storming ideas, contributing information, creating the project and presenting the project.

Evaluation
    Ah-ha! Your project will be evaluated on
  1) how well you described the event's location and the influences it had
  2) how interesting and unique your presentation is
  3) how accurate the information is
  4) how well you worked together

Where On Earth?

It used to take 14 hours to get from Chicago to Zug, Switzerland. These days, you can cross the Atlantic in under three hours. You can send messages across the world at the speed of light. You can turn on a computer and in seconds, learn about the Triple Lakes Trail in Denali or about the murky waters of the Bering Strait. Technology has made the world a smaller place but...geography still covers a lot of ground. Knowledge of places remains essential to social studies education so that students *"can use that knowledge for personal enlightenment and development, and to apply it in making important personal decisions and in participating intelligently in societal decision making that affects our lives"* (Natoli and Gritzner 1988). Where On Earth? takes kids further than simply knowing where Burma is. It will help them understand why places are where they are, what these places are like and how they related to people and to other places. As students work in groups of three, we hope it opens their eyes to the wonder of it all. Just go ask Alice.

Materials

transparencies
transparency markers
transparency erasers, paper towels, cleaning cloths
copies of the map reproducibles

Directions

1. Divide your students into groups of three.
2. Assign roles:
   Facilitator- This team member reinforces the idea that all ideas are O.K. He also makes sure that members stay on task.
   Recorder/Artist- This team member is responsible for recording, charting and drawing the group's ideas.
   Reader- This team member is responsible for keeping the ideas flowing. He shares the group's findings with the class.
3. Present the task. *"Your task today is to explore some of the more interesting features of the earth. We know that one region is different from another because each is characterized by unique features. In your groups of three, share what you know about the different attributes geographers use to identify regions."*

4. Have groups share their ideas. Make a list. *"What we know about regions can help us explain the differences and similarities among various features on earth."*

5. Distribute the materials. Which map fits your instructional objective?

6. Explain the activity. What features do you want students to represent, explore, compare, evaluate, illustrate and label? *"Place the transparency on top of the map. Use the markers to help you show why you think petroleum is abundant in the Gulf Coastal Plain but lacking in the Central Lowlands. Use colors, shapes, symbols, words and pictures to help you explain your theories."*

7. Circulate. Intervene when necessary. Reinforce positive interactions. *"I like the way your group is listening to your ideas, Pat."*

8. Have each reader share. *"Who wants to go first? What helped your group work together?"*

9. *"How did you decide to draw the Missouri River as a super highway? What do you feel you absolutely know for sure about the Coteau Des Prairies?"* Record groups' responses on big paper for display. Use it as a reference.

10. We recommend using the Bloom Taxonomy of Educational Objectives to help you create questions that will catch your students' interest. Pick and choose from these examples. Watch your kids fiddle, play and apply their knowledge. *"Use the map, transparency and markers to show what you know about geography. Create pictures, symbols, colors, labels and so on to..."*

    a. *Prove that the Chesapeake Bay is reaching into the coastal lowlands.*

    b. *Predict the future of the land surrounding the Olympics.*

    c. *Show what happens at the site of the San Andreas Fault.*

    d. *Develop a key that illustrates the ages of the mountain ranges of North America.*

    e. *Illustrate the effects of the eruption and explosion of Mt. St. Helens. Show how other places were involved in the event.*

    f. *Predict the future of Cape Cod.*

Where On Earth?

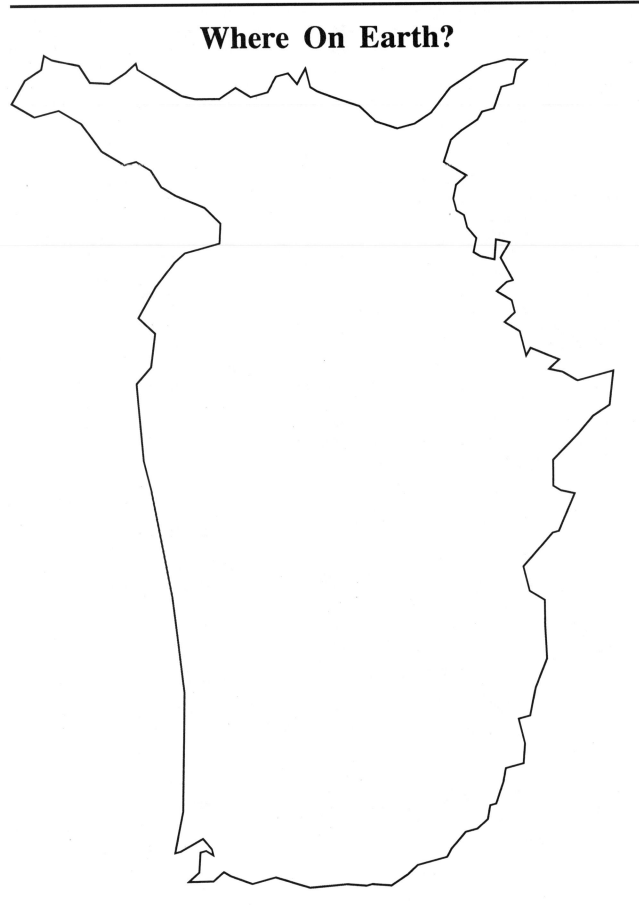

Where On Earth?

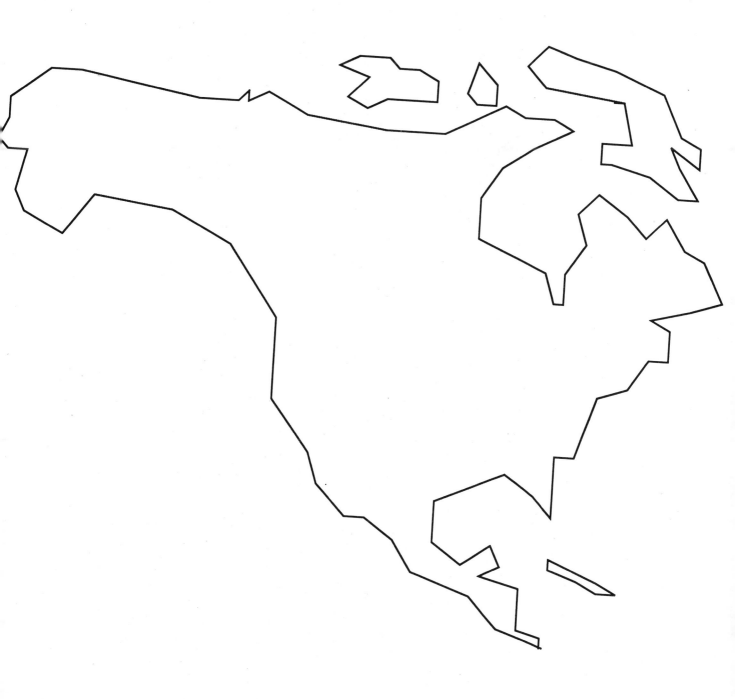

Where On Earth?

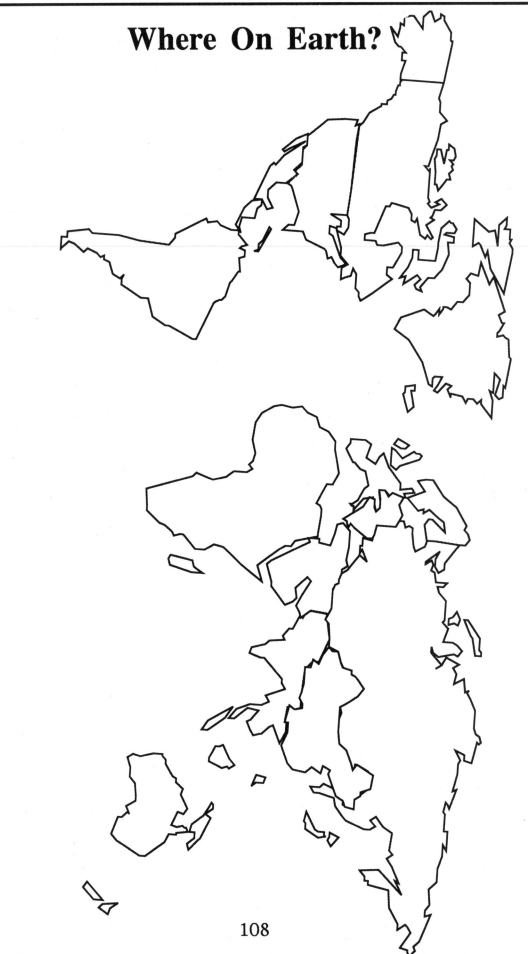

Global View

Spin. Consider. Stop. You're not just looking for a game. You're looking for a game that helps kids learn by experimenting first-hand. You don't want predictable answers. You want unlikely, improbable, impossible, uncertain out-comes. You don't want straight thinking. You want to infuse critical and creative thinking into geography instruction. This activity for two or more players is thinking-centered learning.

Materials

brass fasteners
tagboard (cut into circles, 3" in diameter)
tagboard squares
glue
masking tape
scissors
copies of A Global View reproducibles

Directions

1. Divide your class into pairs.
2. Make spinners. Here's how. Each group needs a brass fastener, a tagboard circle and pointer, 3 or 4 tagboard squares, glue, scissors and a copy of the reproducible. First, ask them to cut out the appropriate earth shape reproducible and past it to the tagboard circle. Assembling the spinner is easy (see illustrations).
3. Explain the game. *"The object of this game is to spin the continent until it you get the direction right. Which country should be on top? How can you describe 'on top' using real navigation terms? What one should be down there? Talk it over. Share your ideas, explorers."*
4. Meet with groups. Help them focus their attention in different directions by asking *what-if* questions and exploring alternative points of view. Pose authentic problems with real-world significance. *"What if Africa switched places with Canada?"*
5. Have partners share their experiences. *"Who wants to go first? Why do you think the Eastern Hemisphere can be described as a region? What connections does the United States have with Canada? Share one discovery you made."*
6. Implement group processing. *"How did working with a partner help you think through the location of Australia? How did you share the responsibility for making the spinner?"*

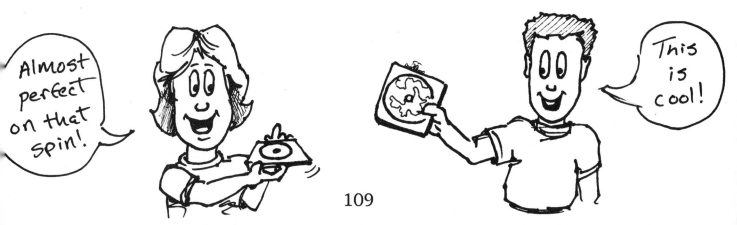

7. Have students make lots of spinners using the different shapes.

8. Generate questions that help students acquire a different perspective of the concepts they understand.

    a. Describe the way in which the continents are like puzzle shapes.

    b. What continents seem to fit together? How can you explain this?

    c. Give verbal directions to go from _____ to _____.

    d. What if the continent of North America were switched? Name at least 3 ways your life would be different. Challenge- name at least 3 positive and 3 negative effects.

    e. Position the continent of _____ correctly. Describe at least 5 ways people have adapted to their environment. Now spin it the wrong way. Talk about the options for natural resources people would have available to them.

    f. Color the continents of _____. Identify the criteria you used for your color choices.

    g. Locate _____ in comparison to _____.

A Global View
Seven Shapes of the World

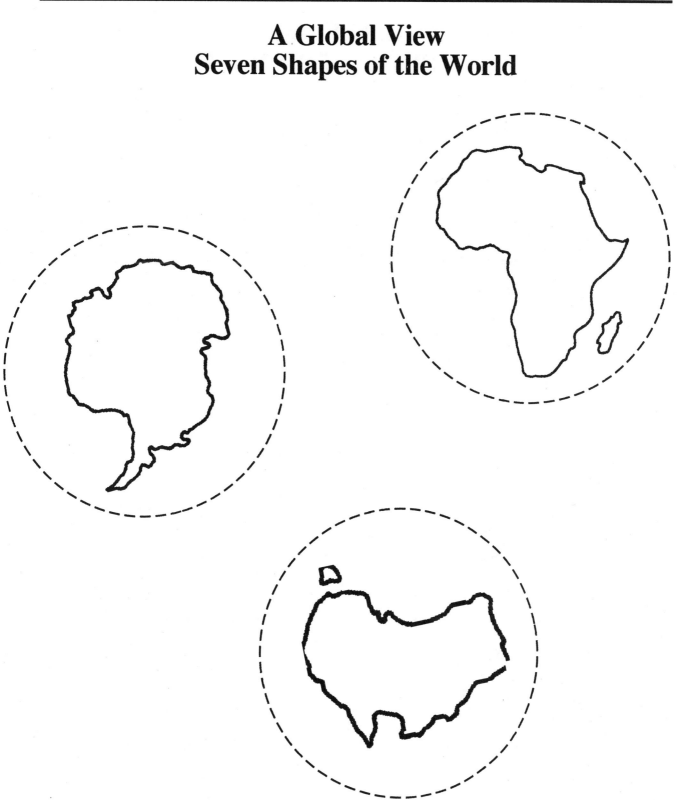

A Global View
Seven Shapes of the World

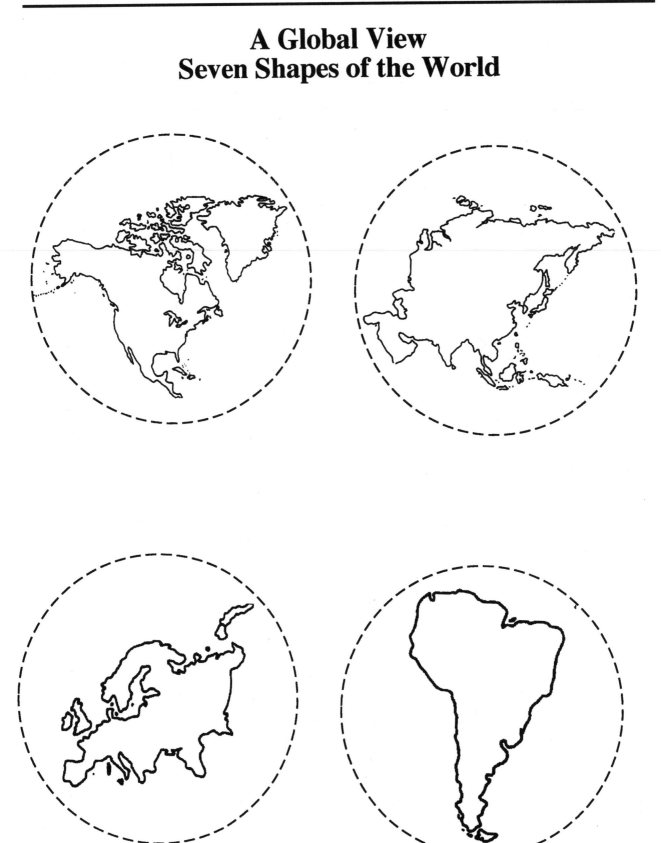

Chapter Five
Science, Cooperative Games and Activities

There is no law that says children...

*can't learn about life from a turtle

*can't snoop, sneak and sleuth to track down a cookie culprit

*shall not study a sunset or train butterflies

*can't crack the genetic code

*may not play Balance of Power

*must learn abstractions rather than scientific *concepts*

*can't *use, know* and *do* science

*absolutely must not be scientifically *creative* or *inventive*

*can't use their *skills, experience & prior knowledge* to learn about science

*can't learn science *actively* & *together*

These laws do not apply. The laws are different here. Chapter Five offers a collection of fresh ideas to help children think like scientists- to identify the problem(s), to ask questions to form theories, to collect and organize information, to test hypotheses, to take risks, to make inferences, to make surveys, to draw conclusions and to have a good, cooperative time doing it.

Cracking the Genetic Code

Cracking the Genetic Code is all about patterns of inheritance. The way we look depends partly on the combinations of genes inside each cell of our bodies. Each of our parents handed down exactly one-half of this information. These genes are like blueprints. According to these blueprints, we could have a widow's peak and freckles, or blue eyes and short lashes and a nice big smile. In this activity, students in groups of two or more make a survey to investigate the question of *"Which characteristics are more common- dominant or recessive?"*

Materials

pencils
copies of the Cracking the Genetic Code reproducible

Directions

1. Divide your class into groups of two. You might want to assign roles or have students self-assign:
  Genealogist- Records information.
  Sensor- Validates the information.
2. Explain the task. *"This activity is for all of you who want to learn more about you body and appreciate its miraculous design. We're going to collect information about how we look."*
3. Discuss patterns of inheritance. *"Traits are features like eye color, hair color, dimples, freckles, eyelashes and earlobes. Traits have different ways of showing up. Some traits are dominant over others. What does the word dominant mean to you? Think about it and share your ideas with your partners. Where have you heard it before?"* Etc.
4. Discuss and list students' ideas.

114

5. "A dominant gene that can be passed on to you from you parents is dimples. How many of you have dimples?"

6. Distribute the reproducible. Explain the process. "This will help you collect information about the question we're investigating. We'll be able to draw conclusions about recessive or dominant genes from our observations. You might be surprised at the results."

7. Monitor each group's progress. Facilitate their learning by reinforcing the idea of a good sample. "Jim's group observed 23 kids. How did you find so many?"

8. Locate and suggest other pertinent literature, filmstrips, experts, etc.

9. Ask groups to explain their conclusions. "Are recessive or dominant traits more common? How many people had freckles?"

10. "Let's finish this sentence. Dominant traits are _____."

11. "What did you like about your roles? How did the roles help to share the responsibility for this activity? What made it easy?"

12. "Thumbs up for good investigating."

13.* Extend this activity. Have students make graphs. Make a graph that compiles students' results. "Graphs are way to picture information. Let's make some comparisons about our findings."

   Ex. Look! 16 people have blond hair and 2 people have red hair. Only 7 people have brown hair. Even though dark hair is dominant over light hair, more people had the recessive trait for hair color.

Cracking the Genetic Code

Calling all sleuths! It's time to crack the code. Here is an activity that will help you find out why there are six people in your grade with red hair and dimples or why there are no people in your class with a blue eyes <u>and</u> extra-long eyelashes. The answers are out there. It's up to you to find them.

Question: Are dominant traits more common than recessive traits?

<u>Directions</u>

1. Take a survey in your class.
2. Work together to collect information that will help you investigate and make conclusions about different traits.
3. Find at least 18 people to observe.
4. Talk about your observations. Share your ideas. Write about them.

DOMINANT!	Number of People	RECESSIVE!	Number of People
Brown hair		Blonde hair	
Dimples		No dimples	
Freckles		No freckles	
Brown eyes		Blue eyes	
extra-long eye lashes		shorter length	
Widow Peak		Regular hair line	
YOUR OWN			

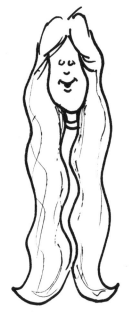

What conclusions can you draw from your survey?

_____

_____

We cracked the genetic code! *Signed,*

_____ & _____

(The scientific method says to observe as many people as you can.)

The Prints Tell The Story

In this activity for groups of four, students learn more about what makes them unique, as well as collecting and analyzing data.

Materials

washable, non-toxic inked stamp pads
paper or index cards
pencils or pens
copies of The Prints Tell The Story reproducibles

Directions

1. Divide your students into groups of four. You might want to assign roles or have students self-assign:

Detective- Inks fingers.
Inspector- Compares & classifies the prints.
FBI- Validates the classifications.
Reporter- Shares results.

2. Introduce the activity. *"Who knows what hospitals do to prevent mix-ups in the nursery? What do police do when they first arrive at the scene of a crime? Turn to the members of your group. Share your ideas."*

3. Have a class discussion. *"Fingerprints are unique. Look at the ridges on your fingers. No one else in this classroom or in the world has the same pattern of ridges on their fingers! Even identical twins have their own sets of one-of-a-kind fingerprints! This activity will help you learn how fingerprints are used as a means of identification and how unique they are."*

4. Distribute the materials. Explain the drill. *"You are about to enter the world of criminal science. Read the directions carefully. Talk about the process. Don't let anyone make off with the goods!"*

5. Circulate. *"Kate's group decided to ink one finger at a time." "See if it helps to press lightly."*

6. Have groups report their findings. Provide feedback. *"Laura's group found that most of their fingerprints were double loops. Wow! They labeled others Unknown. Why do you think so?"*

7. *"Let's finish this sentence. We found out that although it might seem like all our fingers have the same fingerprints_____."* Etc. Have students write their reactions, observations, discoveries in their learning logs.

8. Implement group processing. *"How did you build on each other's observations? How did you reach agreement on fuzzy prints?"*

9. *"Bravo for all criminal scientists!"*

10. *Act it out. WHO DID IT? Have groups choose one person to be the Chief of Detectives. He/she must leave the room. *"Choose a culprit. What crime will he commit? Compose a story to go with the crime. Have him leave his fingerprints at the scene. Use a piece of white paper for the prints. After the crook gets rid of the evidence (washes his hands), ask the detective to return and figure out who did it!"* Make this game even more of a challenge by having the criminal leave only one or two prints at the scene of the crime.

The Prints Tell The Story

Attention all super sleuths. Get ready to enter the world of criminal science. Take a look at the little ridges on your fingers. Fortunately, for snoops, sneaks and detectives, your fingerprints are unique. No one else in the world has the same patterns of ridges on their fingers. No one else has the same footprints either, but that's a different story.

The Investigation: How are fingerprints sorted and classified?
What patterns do my fingerprints have?

Directions

1. Make fingerprint cards. Each person needs 2 cards- one for each hand. Hint- labels are important.
2. Time for fingerprinting. Press each finger, first on the stamp pad and then in each square.
3. Make a complete set for both hands.
4. Now look at you fingerprints and compare them with the patterns shown in the chart. Is each print a whorl, an arch, a double loop, a tented arch? Talk about your decisions with the members in your group. Mark your prints with the first letter of the pattern type.
5. What are all those squiggly lines about? In what ways are they like a map? What do your fingerprints have in common with the rest of your group's? Talk about your ideas. Write about them.

The Prints Tell The Story

sniff sniff sniff

Here they are. They all have names. They're wavy. They have ups and downs. They squiggle. They're called patterns of ridges or print types. Which brings us to...

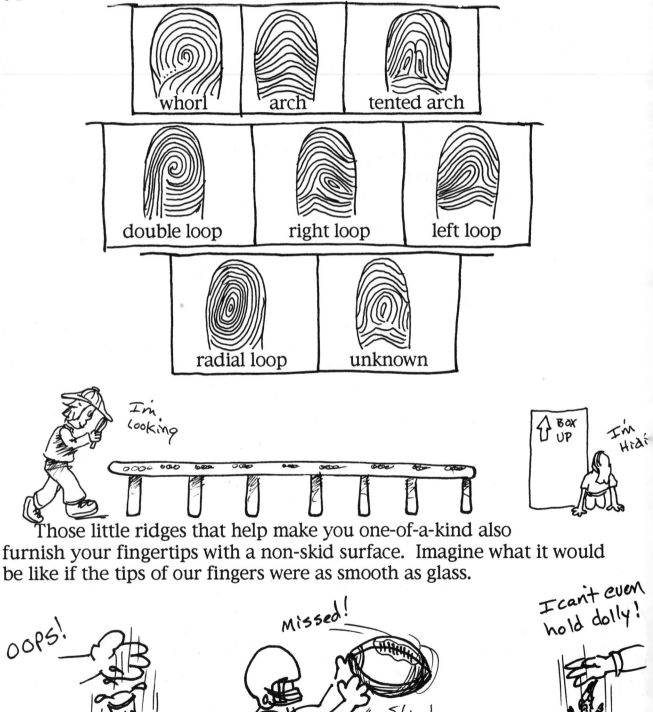

whorl

arch

tented arch

double loop

right loop

left loop

radial loop

unknown

I'm looking

BOX UP

I'm Hidi

Those little ridges that help make you one-of-a-kind also furnish your fingertips with a non-skid surface. Imagine what it would be like if the tips of our fingers were as smooth as glass.

oops!

DROP

Missed!

Slip!

I can't even hold dolly!

 Ahh!

Foodworks

 sniff

You either believe or don't in the separation of church and state or of architecture and decoration but of smell and taste? The olfactory center and the taste center are all part of a package deal. Foodworks proves that point- deliciously. This activity for groups of two also provides experience with collecting and analyzing data and in making generalizations.

Materials

Station I- Mapping Your Tongue
* forks, toothpicks or cotton swabs
* sugar & salt water
* instant coffee or tea
* paper cups
* containers

Station II- Taste Bud Trouble
* apples, pears, carrots, onions, salt
    broccoli, potato and other fruits
    and vegetables
* paper cups
* blindfolds (handkerchiefs)
* forks, toothpicks or cotton swabs

Station III- Taste Bud Tryouts!
* ice cubes
* vegetable-based food dyes
* processed fruits & vegetables
* paper cups
* forks, toothpicks or cotton swabs
* timers or stopwatches

*copies of the **Foodworks** activity sheet reproducibles (stapled into booklets)

Directions
1. Organize the stations. Have pitchers of sugar, salt and vinegar water available at Station I as well as pitchers of diluted coffee or tea. Cut the foods listed for Station II into bite-sized pieces. You need at least 5 different foods. Add food colorings to different processed fruits and vegetables at Station III. Identify the foods by making a key. You need at least 5 different types. Each station can be a cluster of desks, a counter or an available table. Mark each with a sign suspended from the ceiling or propped on an easel.
2. Copy the activity sheet reproducibles. Make covers. Staple into booklets for each child.
3. Organize your class into groups of two.
4. *"Bagels! Quesadillas! French toast! Pizza!"* Raise your hands if you love to eat! What is the fun of eating all about? Think of many answers to this question. Share your ideas with your group."
5. Introduce the tasks. *"You won't find a tuna casserole, lasagna or taco delight at our little restaurants. What you will find are little tests to help you learn some interesting facts about how you taste your food. Get those taste-testers ready."*

Take your students on a tour of each station. Give specific directions for your expectations. *"You will be able to choose the order in which to do these experiments. Please remember that you have to complete all of them. If one restaurant is full, what could you do?"* Etc.

6. Present and discuss the activity booklet.

7. Suggest ways to complete each task. *"Your group is responsible for learning at least (3) facts about how you taste your food. You are expected to talk about the jobs at each station, decide what's important and what it means. Encourage each other. Be able to explain what you understand about the results for each test."*

8. Circulate. *"How's it going? Did you make any predictions before you started?"*
9. Groups of two should evaluate each other's booklets. *"How can your partner's records be improved? Is there any information missing? Is the data clear?"*
10. Ask groups to report their observations and conclusions. *"How important is your sense of smell? Sight? In what ways do your taste buds respond to different tastes?"* Etc.
11. Implement group processing. *"Did you offer and give help? Did you praise someone else? What positive comments did your group use?"*
12. *"Bravo for all official tasters!"*
13. Try a variation for these tests- Compare tasting dry sugar or salt to salt or sugar water. Use a timer or stopwatch.

Mapping Your Tongue

How do you like your chili? Hot? Mild? There are thousands of tiny taste buds spread out on your tongue. You even have a few on the roof of your mouth and surprise, in your pharynx and epiglottis. Taste buds are specialized cells that are connected by sensory nerves to your brain. When chili hits the surface of your tongue, it wakes up the taste buds. *"Action!"* Then, the nerves carry the message to your brain. Your brain lets you know what you're tasting. *"Hot!!!!!"* It's an incredible system. This experiment will help you learn how your taste buds respond to the 4 different tastes- sweet, bitter, sour and salty.

Question: Where are the taste cells located on my tongue?

Directions

1. Dab a bit of sugar water on the back, front, middle and two sides of your partner's tongue.
2. Which part of your partner's tongue tastes the sugar's sweetness? Record your partner's answer by writing the word sweet on the map of a tongue.
3. Do the same test with the other solutions. Use clean swabs. Have your partner rinse his/her mouth between tests.
4. Do you think the map of your tongue will be grouped into the same 4 parts?
5. Repeat testing all 4 solutions but this time reverse roles. You're the official taster.
6. Compare the maps of your tongues? Are they the same? Is there an area of the tongue that is not sensitive to any kind of tastes? Label it.
7. Talk about the results of this test. What can you say about the different parts of the tongue?

Thpptt!

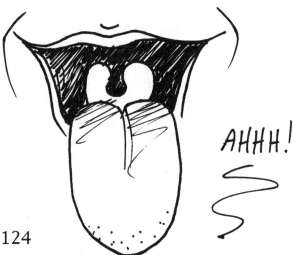

AHHH!

124

hhchoo!

Taste Bud Trouble

What happens to your sense of taste when you have a cold? **Is your sense of taste effected by your sense of smell? What about your sense of sight? Is your sense of smell important to just a few foods or many?** You'll find the answers to these questions and more in this experiment.

Directions

1. Help your partner place a blindfold around his/her head. Tell him or her to pinch his or her nose.
2. Feed your partner a piece of one of the foods. Ask, *"What do you think it is?"*
3. Record your partner's guess.
4. Do this for each different food. Have your partner rinse his or her mouth between tastes.
5. Repeat testing all the foods but this time reverse roles. You're the official taster.
6. Talk about the results of this test. How many foods did your partner guess correctly? How many foods did you get right? How important do you think the sense of smell is in tasting foods? What about the sense of sight?

Name of Food	Guess!	Right? Wrong?

Extra for Experts Try this test again, but don't pinch your nose or have your partner pinch his or her nose. Try it without the blindfold, too. What happens? How are the results affected?

Taste Bud Tryouts!!

Does color affect your sense of taste? What about coldness or dryness? Here's an unusual chance to give your tongue a tryout and find out.

Directions

1. First, use a toothpick or a swab to feed your partner one of the colored foods.
2. What does your partner think it is? Record your partner's guess on the chart.
4. Do the same test with the other foods. Have him or her rinse his or her mouth each time. Don't peek to see what the foods are.
5. Repeat all the steps but this time reverse roles. You do the tasting. Have your partner record your answers.
6. Ta-Da!!! Do you think that the colors of these foods affected sense of taste? Talk about it with your partner. Then, use the key to see if your guesses were right. Well, were they? Were your guesses way off? Explain the results.

NAME OF FOOD	GUESS	RIGHT? WRONG?

How long does it take to taste sugar when your tongue is dry?	Time
How long does it take to taste a food when your tongue is cold?	

7. What about your sense of taste & dryness or coldness? Try this. Both of you stick your tongues out to dry off. HA! We're serious. Have the timer ready. When they're dry, start the timer and take turns putting some sugar on the tips of each other's tongues. How long does it take to taste the sugar? Did you taste it right away? Why do you think so? Record the results.

8. Last, put an ice cube in your mouth for just a few minutes. Use the timer. Take the ice cube out of your mouth and taste one of the colorful foods. Use the timer again to see how long it takes to taste the food. Did you taste it right away? Why do you think so? Record the results.

What did you learn from these tests? What do your results prove? Talk about it. Share your ideas. Be ready to explain what you think.

Balance of Power

Energy. Drama. Interactions. Simulations. Systems. Snack time. Cooperation. It's all here in the Balance of Power game. This activity for groups of 6 or more provides experience with a food chain, as well as thinking strategically.

Materials

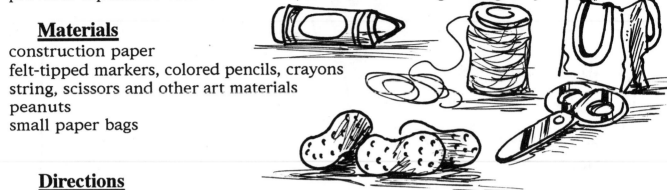

construction paper
felt-tipped markers, colored pencils, crayons
string, scissors and other art materials
peanuts
small paper bags

Directions

*This game needs space! Find an big area where you can also make a mess.
1. Bring on the prerequisite information. Immerse your students in the theme of interactions or systems. Use a myriad of resources including guest speakers, films, non-fiction, etc.
2. Elicit students' knowledge of food chains. Make a web to represent their ideas. Ex. *"Where do all food chains begin?"* From this information, determine a food chain to investigate.
3. Divide your students into groups of (6). Divide the number of students in your class by the number of animals in the food chain you want to simulate.
4. Explain the task. *"Today we're going to play a game to see what happens in the _____ food chain. How does it play out in the balance of nature? Who survives? Why? How? Etc."* Assign an animal to each group.

5. *"In your groups, discuss everything you know about your animal. Think about what it eats, its food sources, its contributions to a food chain, etc."* If time permits, groups can web, list or write about their ideas.

6. Have each group share their information.

7. Distribute construction paper (one color) to each group as well as scissors, markers, string, etc. *"Make signs that identify what animal you will represent. Make sure that you label your signs, front and back with the name of the animal you're playing..."*

8. Give each player a paper bag. *"This is to hold your food."*

9. Let the game begin. Take your class to the selected site. Spread peanuts around and give directions. *"This is the food for the (grasshoppers). When I say, 'Go!' all (grasshoppers) must try to collect as much food as they can. The catch is that when the (grasshoppers) are hopping, so are the (frogs). (Frogs), you are to tag as many (grasshoppers) as you can. If you tag a (grasshopper), the (grasshopper) has to give up his or her food and come over here to the graveyard. The (grasshopper) is out of the game. The same rules apply to (frogs). You are being pursued by (snakes) which are being hunted by (hawks)."* Adapt these directions to the food chain you're investigating.

10. Designate the playing field boundaries. Decide on the time limit. Five minutes is good or... when all the (grasshoppers) have been eaten.

11. *"Time!"* At the end of the game, ask each group to get together and count the food (peanuts) collected. *"How do you account for collecting the largest number of peanuts?"*

12. Next, count the number of survivors. Record the results. Make a graph.

13. *"What do you know now that you didn't know before? What do you notice about the numbers of survivors? Is there a balance? Did some animals from each group make it? Why do you think so? What about the food? Which animal has the largest number? Talk it over in your groups. What conclusions can we draw from the results of Balance of Power? Could similar results happen in the real world?"*

14. Challenge your students to create variations for this game. Have them play the game again, switching their place in the food chain. *"Frogs become hawks, grasshoppers become frogs, etc."*

Jeopardy

Collaboration. Understanding performances. Infusion of critical and creative thinking. Fun. "What do I want from a game that will help my students think about the science content they are learning?" Our point is. Sometimes you need answers first, not questions.

Materials

a myriad of resources including old magazines
felt-tipped markers, colored pencils, pens
scissors
glue
copies of the Jeopardy gameboard reproducible

Directions

1. Write the topic as the gameboard title. Determine four categories that relate to the content you want students to understand, review, and learn. Write them at the top of the column on the reproducible. Then, make enough copies so that each group of partners in your class has one gameboard.
2. Divide your students into groups of four. Students pair off within their groups.
3. Explain the task. *"What question can you ask from this information? It's a sphere. It's a rock flying through space. Every 10 seconds 45 people are born here. Etc. The object of this game is to ask a question based on information that your teammates will write. You know a lot about.......Now we're going to extend and share our knowledge. Each group of partners will write answers to complete a gameboard. Then you will exchange the gameboard with the other pair in your group. You have to write questions for the answers."*
4. Distribute materials to each pair.
5. *"Partners, write 4 answers for each category. Use pictures and drawings to make your answers different. Try to challenge your teammates by trying new ideas. "* Draw a gameboard and scoring chart on the board to further help you explain the process.
6. Monitor each group's progress. Encourage students to create visuals as well as to write.
7. Have the partners reunite and exchange gameboards. *"Write questions for your teammates' answers. Share your ideas. Consult with each other. Decide what's important."*

Get technical, think of non-examples. Use pictures from magazines! How about a statistic? Try names!

8. Within the group, partners share and discuss the finished gameboards. *"Explain your ideas. Take turns. Make sure that all four of you agree on the questions. If you don't agree, figure it out. Is the answer given just another point of view? If you're really stuck, ask me for help."*

9. Discuss the process. *"What did you learn from this activity? How did you share the work?"*

10. *"I liked the way partners explained their thinking to each other."*

131

Jeopardy

This gameboard is a tool, not just a sheet of paper. Draw on it. Write on it. Cut and paste pictures of things on it. When you are done you just might know a lot more than you thought about...

← The topic!!

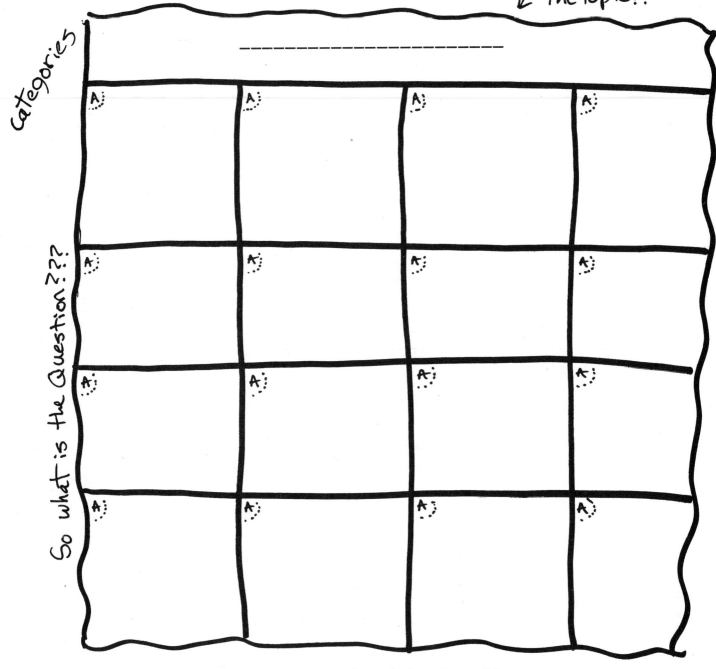

The answers were conceived and developed by _____ and _____. The questions were conceived and developed by _____ and _____. Such expertise. Such fun. Such knowledge.

Bird's- Eye View

The theme of interaction takes a new path. Neither outdated or gimmicky, Bird's-Eye View approaches the familiar concept of camouflage in an original way.

Materials

jelly beans, hard candy, macaroni spirals, wooden cubes (any multi-colored assortment of small objects)
copies of the Bird's-Eye View reproducible
pencils
stopwatch or timer

Directions

* This game should be played outdoors in a grassy area. Just before you play Bird's- Eye View, sprinkle, spread and strew the candy or macaroni over the grass. Scatter some on any surrounding surface areas, too.

1. Organize a wealth of materials- books, posters, videos, charts, filmstrips and anything you can find related to protective adaptations into a research center. Schedule field trips to zoos. Arrange for guest speakers to visit. Address a wide variety of objectives so that students have many opportunities to understand the large concept.

2. Divide your students into groups of three. Assign roles:
    The Guide- Records information.
    The Reporter- Reports to the class.
    The Manager- Keeps the group on track and keeps track of the
      numbers of animals found on the hunt.

3. In their groups of three, ask students to describe a polar bear, a woodchuck, a robin, a grasshopper, etc. Then, ask students if the way the animal looks has anything to do with its habitat. After students discuss their examples, explain that the _____blending into its surroundings is an example of camouflage. Etc.

4. Introduce the game. *"The object of today's game is to observe how color helps to hide animals from their enemies."*

5. Take the students outdoors. Review the rules. Show students a jelly bean, a spiral or whatever object you decided to use to represent 'bugs.' *"You are pigeons, starlings, red-winged blackbirds and finches. You're hungry. It's been a long, hard winter but the bugs have come out! You have to find them! You have 2 minutes. When I say, 'Go!' collect as many bugs as you can find. Then get together with your group, count your bugs and record them on this chart."* Present the reproducible. Have it available on the sidelines as well as writing utensils and something to write on. (It's more effective to hold the class discussion outside.)

6. *"Go!"* Start the clock NOW.

7. Allow groups time to reconvene and record their results. *"Talk about what happened. Which bugs were best camouflaged? Be able to explain your findings."* Etc.

8. Ask groups to share. *"What does your chart show? How many spirals in all did you find? How can you explain it? Did you pick up more of one color than another? What made this color easiest to find? "* Make a class graph that compiles the information. Have them make generalizations as to which bugs are the best camouflaged for this kind of surroundings.

9. Continue the discussion to include how some animals are also camouflaged by textures, shapes, patterns or by unpleasant tastes (often poisonous). Talk about attributes that protect an animal as well as camouflage it such as a turtle's shell.

* This game can be played using other animals in food chains- fish (use dark backgrounds to simulate the ocean or other bodies of water), small rodents and birds of prey, frogs and snakes, butterflies and frogs, etc.

* Play it again. Use a different food or object to explore the effects of shapes or patterns.

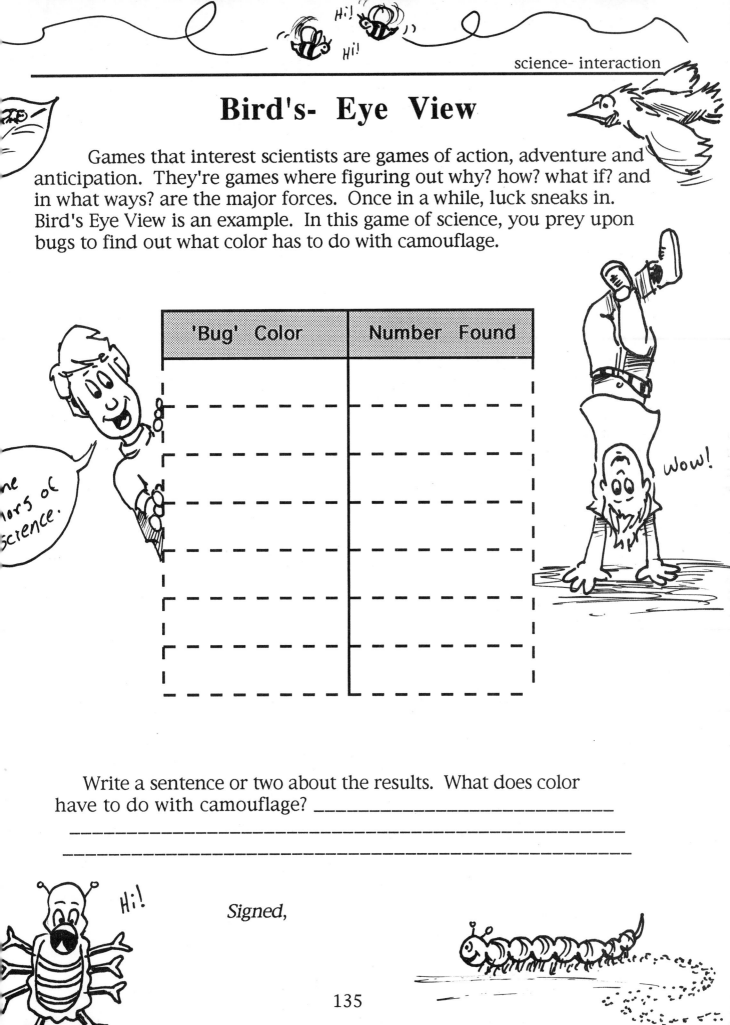

Bird's- Eye View

Games that interest scientists are games of action, adventure and anticipation. They're games where figuring out why? how? what if? and in what ways? are the major forces. Once in a while, luck sneaks in. Bird's Eye View is an example. In this game of science, you prey upon bugs to find out what color has to do with camouflage.

'Bug' Color	Number Found

Write a sentence or two about the results. What does color have to do with camouflage? _____

_____

_____

Signed,

Survival

You remember Freeze Tag. It's one of the world's fastest games. This variation highlights the theme of interaction. In other words, it illustrates "who eats whom" in an ecosystem.

Materials
construction paper

Directions

* Find a site that has 2 goal lines or base areas at either end.

1. Discuss feeding relationships and food chains. *"Grass and trees(producers) are eaten by birds, mice, cows, insects and other animals (herbivores). The herbivores are eaten in turn by frogs, hawks, weasels, foxes, etc. (carnivores)."*

2. Your class, as a whole group, can decide on what 4 (at least) animals they wish to play. At least one producer is needed.

3. Divide your class into (4) groups. Assign an animal to each or have students select.

4. Have groups make signs or hats to wear that identify the plants and animals they'll be playing.

5. Explain the rules. Simple! The producers gather at one of the goal or base line areas. The carnivores stand in the middle of the forest, the ocean or etc. (the playing field). The herbivores have to hop, walk, swim, run across the playing field to get food without being tagged by the carnivores. *"If you're tagged, you've had it."* Designate a spot for the non-survivors to sit.

6. Have groups discuss strategy. *"What will you do? What are your best chances for survival? What disadvantages do you have to overcome?"* Etc.

7. Go outdoors and play!

8. Discuss the outcome of the Survival game. *"Could a similar series of events happen in the real world? Why do you think so? What did you like about your position in this game? What was your link?"* Etc.

9. Implement group processing. *"Did being a member of a group increase your chances of survival? Did you work together? How?"*

10. Note- The carnivores can also be called secondary consumers and the herbivores primary consumers.

Incredible Adaptations

"There's nothing as constant as change." Wasn't it Aristotle who said that? Adaptation is a plant or animal's way of dealing with a changed environment. It's never-ending. In this activity for groups of four, students investigate different structural adaptations and their purposes. It's a fun-filled, process-oriented experience that focuses on the theme of ...you guessed it, interaction. It also connects with social studies and regions.

Materials

Station I- Thumbs Up!
* masking tape
* paper
* pencils
* peanuts

Station II- Beak Bites
* pipe cleaners
* spoons
* rulers
* clothespins
* toothpicks
* paper rolls
* cereal, goldfish crackers, popcorn (You need at least 4 different types of food)
* reference materials

Station III- The Nose Knows
* boxes containing at least 5 objects that give off a strong odor such as: a bottle of vanilla or perfume, lemon juice, mint extract, banana extract, almond extract, garlic, etc.

*copies of the Incredible Adaptations reproducibles

Directions
1. Organize the stations. Each station can be a cluster of desks, a counter or an available table. Mark each with a sign suspended from the ceiling or propped on an easel.
2. Copy the activity sheet reproducibles. Staple into booklets for each child.
3. Organize your class into groups of four.
4. Discuss ways in which different animals have adapted for seeing, sensing, eating, hiding and defense. Ex. *"Look at this picture. How is the otter adapted for life in the ocean? What about the walrus? Compare the adaptations of these two animals. Talk about the ways in which they are the same and the ways in which they are different. Share your ideas. Explain how you think each animal is adapted for seeing, sensing, eating, hiding and defending itself."* Etc.

5. Have groups report to the class. *"Which group wants to go first? How did you decide to make lists? Does anyone else have an observation to offer?"*

6. Introduce the tasks. *"You are going to investigate different adaptations."*

7. Present and discuss the activity booklet. *"Use it to record your findings and to guide your through each investigation."* Tour the three stations. Set expectations. *"Work together. Talk about what you think is going to happen when you do the experiment. Ask questions if you don't understand. Decide if it reminds you of anything else."* Etc.

8. Have groups rotate from one station to another at their own pace.

9. Circulate. *"How's it going? What did you predict?"*

10. Groups of four should evaluate each other's booklets. *"Can you offer any suggestions for improvement? Is the data clear?"* Etc.

11. Ask groups to share their results. Encourage them speculate about how each adaptation investigated helps different organisms. *"How do our opposable thumbs help us? Can you think of another animal with this adaptation?"* Etc.

12. Implement group processing. *"What did you do to help your group complete this task? Colossal understandings were reached today!"*

Thumbs Up!

For this investigation you need to know what an opposable thumb is. Look at your thumbs. Where are they? *"Opposite my fingers!"* Right! Humans have opposable thumbs that enable us to do things. *"Like what?"* This investigation will help you see the usefulness of this adaptation.

Directions

1. Have a member of your group tape your thumbs to your hands. Use masking tape.
2. Now try to do the following tasks with your thumbs taped. Record what happened.
3. Do the same tasks with your thumbs free. Record how each task went.
4. Talk about the results with your group. What surprised you? What do you know now that you didn't know before?

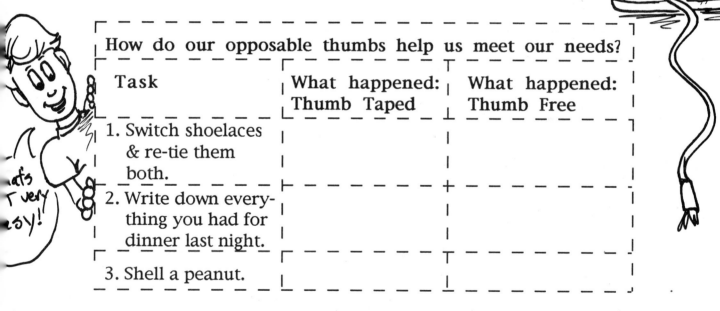

How do our opposable thumbs help us meet our needs?		
Task	What happened: Thumb Taped	What happened: Thumb Free
1. Switch shoelaces & re-tie them both.		
2. Write down everything you had for dinner last night.		
3. Shell a peanut.		

5. Write about the experience.

_____

_____

_____

Beak Bites

Name a bird. Each member of your group has to name a different species. Each of these birds is adapted, or formed, for seeing, sensing, eating, hiding and defending itself. In this investigation, you're going to discover how a bird's beak helps it catch food.

Directions

1. Look over the different materials at this station.
2. Use them to build a model of a bird's beak.
3. Use it to pick up food.
4. Record your findings.
5. Talk about the results. What can you conclude from this investigation? How is a bird adapted for obtaining food?

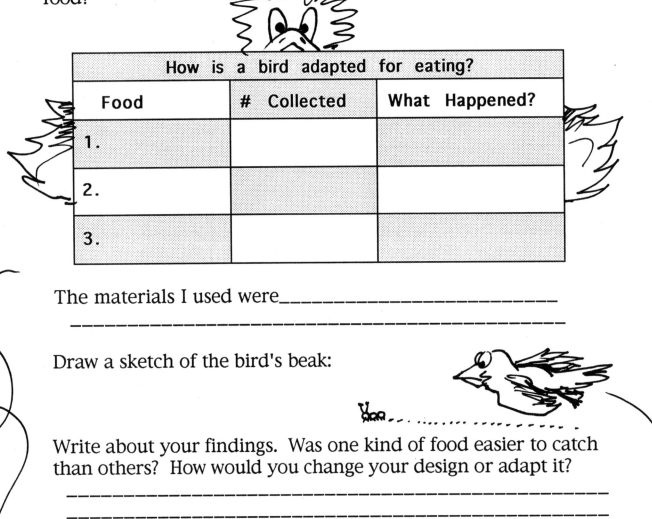

How is a bird adapted for eating?		
Food	# Collected	What Happened?
1.		
2.		
3.		

The materials I used were_____

_____

Draw a sketch of the bird's beak:

Write about your findings. Was one kind of food easier to catch than others? How would you change your design or adapt it?

_____

_____

The Nose Knows

Many animals' sense of smell helps them detect its prey or to detect danger. In this investigation, you'll discover the relationship between sense of smell and memory. These centers are close together in the brain.

Question: How does a sense of smell help an animal obtain food?

Directions:
1. Take the objects out of the box at this station.
2. Pass them around to the other members of your group.
3. Have one person put them back into the box.
4. Now, write down what you saw.
5. Compare your results. Does your list agree with everyone else's? What's missing? What extra did you add?
6. What did you find out about your sense of smell and your memory?

I saw and smelled......

_____

_____

_____

_____

_____

_____

Write about your findings. _____

_____

Cool Cubes

Save the airfare to Reykjavik, Yellowknife, Nome. The science of ice is here. On this page. Cool Cubes is organized around the theme of energy. It will challenge students' critical and creative thinking skills as they work in groups of three.

Materials

ice cubes
containers (milk, yogurt, cottage cheese..)
stopwatches or timers
vegetable-based food coloring

Directions

*Determine an area for the melt-down.
* Make colored ice cubes. Each group of three needs 1 ice cube in a container.
1. Elicit students' understanding and knowledge of heat energy, solids and liquids. *"When is water a solid? In what other forms can water appear? What happens to water when it is heated? What happens to popsicles when they are near heat?"* Etc.
2. Introduce the activity. *"Today we're going to investigate the best way to change a solid to a liquid."*
3. Divide your class into groups of three. Show students an ice cube in a container. *"What kinds of things might make this ice cube melt? Surprise yourself by finding out how long it will take to melt it. Think of some strategies. What can you do with it? Share your ideas with your group. The catch is that the ice cube has to stay in the container. No part of your body can touch it."*
4. Ask groups to predict how much time it will take them to melt their cubes. *"Why do you think so?"*
5. Explain the rules. *"We're going to go (outdoors to the playground) for the icy event. Keep track of the time. Work together to find a way to melt your ice cubes in record-breaking time."*

6. Distribute the ice cubes and stopwatches and go for it. *"Start the timers NOW!"*
7. Circulate. Encourage students to use what they know about dark and light colors, light absorption, body heat, etc.
8. Have groups share their results. *"Were your predictions right on? Way off? Why do you think so? In what ways is heat a form of energy? What strategies did you use? What do you know about heat energy that you didn't know before this activity?"*
9. Implement group processing. *"How did you share the work? What would you do differently the next time?"*
10. *"Congratulations! You melted ice cubes, learned about heat energy and had a good time doing it."*
11. Extend this activity. Give each group a piece of string (8" long), a colored ice cube, salt and a glass jar. *"Here's another mystery! Can you lift an ice cube out of water? The catch is that you can only use one end of a piece of string. Talk about it in your groups."* Distribute the glass jars. Have one student from each group fill it 3/4 full of water. Give each group a piece of string, a colored ice cube and some salt. *"Carefully drop the ice cube in the water. Lay one end of the string on it. Sprinkle a little salt over the ice cube. Wait a few minutes. What happens when you lift the string?"* Have groups discuss the results. *"What effect did the salt have? What did you notice happening to the ice cube when you sprinkled the salt on it? What do you know about using salt in cold, icy weather?"* Etc.

References

Aronson, E. *The Jigsaw Classroom*. Beverly Hills, Ca.: Sage Publications, 1978.

Bruner, Jerome. *On Knowing: Essays for the Left Hand*. New York, New York: Athenaeum, 1965.

Gardner, Howard. *Frames of Mind: The Theory of Multiple Intelligences*. New York, New York: Basic Books, Inc., 1983.

Kagan, Spencer. *Cooperative Learning Resources for Teachers*. San Juan Capistrano, Ca.: Resources for Teachers, 1989.

Lyman, Frank and J. McTighe. "Cueing Thinking in the Classroom: The Promise of Theory-Embedded Tools." *Educational Leadership* 45, April, 1988.

National Council of Teachers of Mathematics. *Curriculum and Evaluation Standards for School Mathematics*. Reston, VA.: 1989.

Natoli, Salvatore J. and Charles F. Gritzner. "Modern Geography." *Strengthening Geography In The Social Studies*. Washington, DC.: National Council For The Social Studies, 1988.